CHINESE NAMES, SURNAM
LOCATIONS & ADDRESSES

中国大陆地址集

GUANGXI ZHUANG AUTONOMOUS REGION - PART 10

广西壮族自治区

ZIYUE TANG

汤子玥

ACKNOWLEDGEMENT

I am deeply indebted to my friends and family members to support me throughout my life. Without their invaluable love and guidance, this work wouldn't have been possible.

Thank you

Ziyue Tang

汤子玥

PREFACE

The book introduces foreigner students to the Chinese names along with locations and addresses from the **Guangxi Zhuang Autonomous Region** of China (中国广西壮族自治区). The book contains 150 entries (names, addresses) explained with simplified Chinese characters, pinyin and English.

Chinese names follow the standard convention where the given name is written after the surname. For example, in 王威 (Wang Wei), Wang is the surname, and Wei is the given name. Further, the surnames are generally made of one (王) or two characters (司马). Similarly, the given names are also made of either one or two characters. For example, 司马威 (Sima Wei) is a three character Chinese name suitable for men. 司马威威 is a four character Chinese name.

Chinese addresses are comprised of different administrative units that start with the largest geographic entity (country) and continue to the smallest entity (county, building names, room number). For example, a typical address in Nanjing city (capital of Jiangsu province) would look like 江苏省南京市清华路 28 栋 520 室 (Jiāngsū shěng nánjīng shì qīnghuá lù 28 dòng 520 shì; Room 520, Building 28, Qinghua Road, Nanjing City, Jiangsu Province).

CONTENTS

CHAPTER 1: NAME, SURNAME & ADDRESSES (1-30)

1351。姓名: 房先秀

住址（火车站）：广西壮族自治区崇左市龙州县勇山路 769 号崇左站（邮政编码：967870）。联系电话：36012352。电子邮箱：qkfns@uwcftnlj.chr.cn

Zhù zhǐ: Fáng Xiān Xiù Guǎngxī Zhuàngzú Zìzhìqū Chóng Zuǒ Shì Lóng Zhōu Xiàn Yǒng Shān Lù 769 Hào Cóng Zuǒ Zhàn (Yóuzhèng Biānmǎ：967870). Liánxì Diànhuà：36012352. Diànzǐ Yóuxiāng：qkfns@uwcftnlj.chr.cn

Xian Xiu Fang, Chongzuo Railway Station, 769 Yong Shan Road, Longzhou County, Chongzuo, Guangxi Autonomous Region. Postal Code: 967870. Phone Number：36012352. E-mail：qkfns@uwcftnlj.chr.cn

1352。姓名: 汪化辉

住址（大学）：广西壮族自治区贺州市钟山县智泽大学中水路 365 号（邮政编码：939294）。联系电话：82683675。电子邮箱：lqnow@lbvgqyma.edu.cn

Zhù zhǐ: Wāng Huā Huī Guǎngxī Zhuàngzú Zìzhìqū Hèzhōu Shì Zhōng Shān Xiàn Zhì Zé DàxuéZhòng Shuǐ Lù 365 Hào (Yóuzhèng Biānmǎ：939294). Liánxì Diànhuà：82683675. Diànzǐ Yóuxiāng：lqnow@lbvgqyma.edu.cn

Hua Hui Wang, Zhi Ze University, 365 Zhong Shui Road, Zhongshan County, Hezhou, Guangxi Autonomous Region. Postal Code: 939294. Phone Number：82683675. E-mail：lqnow@lbvgqyma.edu.cn

1353。姓名: 别亚坚

住址（机场）：广西壮族自治区贺州市平桂区山强路 282 号贺州坡惟国际机场（邮政编码：633510）。联系电话：81910273。电子邮箱：glnhe@fwbasxei.airports.cn

Zhù zhǐ: Bié Yà Jiān Guǎngxī Zhuàngzú Zìzhìqū Hèzhōu Shì Píng Guì Qū Shān Qiáng Lù 282 Hào Hèzōu Pō Wéi Guó Jì Jī Chǎng (Yóuzhèng Biānmǎ：633510). Liánxì Diànhuà：81910273. Diànzǐ Yóuxiāng：glnhe@fwbasxei.airports.cn

Ya Jian Bie, Hezhou Po Wei International Airport, 282 Shan Qiang Road, Pinggui District, Hezhou, Guangxi Autonomous Region. Postal Code: 633510. Phone Number：81910273. E-mail：glnhe@fwbasxei.airports.cn

1354。姓名: 支己晗

住址（公共汽车站）：广西壮族自治区梧州市岑溪市仓庆路 762 号沛焯站（邮政编码：500577）。联系电话：97867489。电子邮箱：ywogb@lmwazrei.transport.cn

Zhù zhǐ: Zhī Jǐ Hán Guǎngxī Zhuàngzú Zìzhìqū Wúzhōu Shì Cénxī Shì Cāng Qìng Lù 762 Hào Pèi Chāo Zhàn (Yóuzhèng Biānmǎ：500577). Liánxì Diànhuà：97867489. Diànzǐ Yóuxiāng：ywogb@lmwazrei.transport.cn

Ji Han Zhi, Pei Chao Bus Station, 762 Cang Qing Road, Cenxi City, Wuzhou, Guangxi Autonomous Region. Postal Code: 500577. Phone Number：97867489. E-mail：ywogb@lmwazrei.transport.cn

1355。姓名: 壤驷愈可

住址（大学）：广西壮族自治区防城港市港口区秀金大学铁敬路 707 号（邮政编码：547174）。联系电话：95946654。电子邮箱：jvesn@lzsefgkp.edu.cn

Zhù zhǐ: Rǎngsì Yù Kě Guǎngxī Zhuàngzú Zìzhìqū Fángchénggǎng Shì Gǎngkǒu Qū Xiù Jīn DàxuéTiě Jìng Lù 707 Hào (Yóuzhèng Biānmǎ：547174). Liánxì Diànhuà：95946654. Diànzǐ Yóuxiāng：jvesn@lzsefgkp.edu.cn

Yu Ke Rangsi, Xiu Jin University, 707 Tie Jing Road, Port Area, Fangchenggang, Guangxi Autonomous Region. Postal Code: 547174. Phone Number：95946654. E-mail：jvesn@lzsefgkp.edu.cn

1356。姓名:怀成懂

住址（医院）：广西壮族自治区贺州市富川瑶族自治县易圣路 702 号鹤盛医院（邮政编码：975558）。联系电话：85977521。电子邮箱：sjrko@xjitnckl.health.cn

Zhù zhǐ: Huái Chéng Dǒng Guǎngxī Zhuàngzú Zìzhìqū Hèzhōu Shì Fùchuān Yáozú Zìzhìxiàn Yì Shèng Lù 702 Hào Hè Chéng Yī Yuàn （Yóuzhèng Biānmǎ：975558）. Liánxì Diànhuà：85977521. Diànzǐ Yóuxiāng：sjrko@xjitnckl.health.cn

Cheng Dong Huai, He Cheng Hospital, 702 Yi Sheng Road, Fuchuan Yao Autonomous County, Hezhou, Guangxi Autonomous Region. Postal Code: 975558. Phone Number：85977521. E-mail：sjrko@xjitnckl.health.cn

1357。姓名: 冉轶威

住址（公司）：广西壮族自治区崇左市扶绥县兆中路 664 号仓成有限公司（邮政编码：617218）。联系电话：67383767。电子邮箱：hcqei@vqdipxfw.biz.cn

Zhù zhǐ: Rǎn Yì Wēi Guǎngxī Zhuàngzú Zìzhìqū Chóng Zuǒ Shì Fú Suí Xiàn Zhào Zhòng Lù 664 Hào Cāng Chéng Yǒuxiàn Gōngsī （Yóuzhèng Biānmǎ：617218）. Liánxì Diànhuà：67383767. Diànzǐ Yóuxiāng：hcqei@vqdipxfw.biz.cn

Yi Wei Ran, Cang Cheng Corporation, 664 Zhao Zhong Road, Fusui County, Chongzuo, Guangxi Autonomous Region. Postal Code: 617218. Phone Number：67383767. E-mail：hcqei@vqdipxfw.biz.cn

1358。姓名: 尤铁毅

住址（酒店）：广西壮族自治区百色市田阳区沛己路 443 号近寰酒店（邮政编码：830535）。联系电话：83823189。电子邮箱：evfit@wibdmpgu.biz.cn

Zhù zhǐ: Yóu Fū Yì Guǎngxī Zhuàngzú Zìzhìqū Bǎisè Shì Tiányáng Qū Bèi Jǐ Lù 443 Hào Jìn Huán Jiǔ Diàn （Yóuzhèng Biānmǎ：830535）. Liánxì Diànhuà：83823189. Diànzǐ Yóuxiāng：evfit@wibdmpgu.biz.cn

Fu Yi You, Jin Huan Hotel, 443 Bei Ji Road, Tianyang District, Baise, Guangxi Autonomous Region. Postal Code: 830535. Phone Number：83823189. E-mail：evfit@wibdmpgu.biz.cn

1359。姓名: 钮强毅

住址（火车站）：广西壮族自治区崇左市江州区勇沛路 273 号崇左站（邮政编码：114385）。联系电话：32708346。电子邮箱：yontu@gzopcvqr.chr.cn

Zhù zhǐ: Niǔ Qiáng Yì Guǎngxī Zhuàngzú Zìzhìqū Chóng Zuǒ Shì Jiāng Zhōu Qū Yǒng Bèi Lù 273 Hào Cóng Zuǒ Zhàn（Yóuzhèng Biānmǎ：114385). Liánxì Diànhuà：32708346. Diànzǐ Yóuxiāng：yontu@gzopcvqr.chr.cn

Qiang Yi Niu, Chongzuo Railway Station, 273 Yong Bei Road, Jiangzhou District, Chongzuo, Guangxi Autonomous Region. Postal Code: 114385. Phone Number：32708346. E-mail：yontu@gzopcvqr.chr.cn

1360。姓名: 湛鸣原

住址（公司）：广西壮族自治区河池市南丹县乐屹路 666 号不坚有限公司（邮政编码：477940）。联系电话：42353899。电子邮箱：fzxhj@ijvybwlp.biz.cn

Zhù zhǐ: Zhàn Míng Yuán Guǎngxī Zhuàngzú Zìzhìqū Héchí Shì Nán Dān Xiàn Lè Yì Lù 666 Hào Bù Jiān Yǒuxiàn Gōngsī（Yóuzhèng Biānmǎ：477940). Liánxì Diànhuà：42353899. Diànzǐ Yóuxiāng：fzxhj@ijvybwlp.biz.cn

Ming Yuan Zhan, Bu Jian Corporation, 666 Le Yi Road, Nandan County, Hechi, Guangxi Autonomous Region. Postal Code: 477940. Phone Number：42353899. E-mail：fzxhj@ijvybwlp.biz.cn

1361。姓名: 权己福

住址（大学）：广西壮族自治区柳州市融水苗族自治县译岐大学顺源路 112 号（邮政编码：313988）。联系电话：11220589。电子邮箱：nexwq@ocnszmte.edu.cn

Zhù zhǐ: Quán Jǐ Fú Guǎngxī Zhuàngzú Zìzhìqū Liǔzhōu Shì Róng Shuǐ Miáozú Zìzhìxiàn Yì Qí DàxuéShùn Yuán Lù 112 Hào（Yóuzhèng Biānmǎ：313988). Liánxì Diànhuà：11220589. Diànzǐ Yóuxiāng：nexwq@ocnszmte.edu.cn

Ji Fu Quan, Yi Qi University, 112 Shun Yuan Road, Rongshui Miao Autonomous County, Liuzhou, Guangxi Autonomous Region. Postal Code: 313988. Phone Number：11220589. E-mail：nexwq@ocnszmte.edu.cn

1362。姓名: 赏桥领

住址（酒店）：广西壮族自治区梧州市万秀区白茂路 183 号学郁酒店（邮政编码：242327）。联系电话：71572893。电子邮箱：ehzmi@fsiabhjm.biz.cn

Zhù zhǐ: Shǎng Qiáo Lǐng Guǎngxī Zhuàngzú Zìzhìqū Wúzhōu Shì Wàn Xiù Qū Bái Mào Lù 183 Hào Xué Yù Jiǔ Diàn（Yóuzhèng Biānmǎ：242327). Liánxì Diànhuà：71572893. Diànzǐ Yóuxiāng：ehzmi@fsiabhjm.biz.cn

Qiao Ling Shang, Xue Yu Hotel, 183 Bai Mao Road, Wanxiu District, Wuzhou, Guangxi Autonomous Region. Postal Code: 242327. Phone Number：71572893. E-mail：ehzmi@fsiabhjm.biz.cn

1363。姓名: 惠惟舟

住址（火车站）：广西壮族自治区柳州市融安县彬领路 263 号柳州站（邮政编码：329753）。联系电话：34332158。电子邮箱：ikdwj@lefxhpgz.chr.cn

Zhù zhǐ: Huì Wéi Zhōu Guǎngxī Zhuàngzú Zìzhìqū Liǔzhōu Shì Róng Ānxiàn Bīn Lǐng Lù 263 Hào Liǔzōu Zhàn（Yóuzhèng Biānmǎ：329753). Liánxì Diànhuà：34332158. Diànzǐ Yóuxiāng：ikdwj@lefxhpgz.chr.cn

Wei Zhou Hui, Liuzhou Railway Station, 263 Bin Ling Road, Rongan County, Liuzhou, Guangxi Autonomous Region. Postal Code: 329753. Phone Number：34332158. E-mail：ikdwj@lefxhpgz.chr.cn

1364。姓名: 单己斌

住址（博物院）：广西壮族自治区贺州市昭平县山德路 846 号贺州博物馆（邮政编码：721205）。联系电话：44700076。电子邮箱：vhslb@lmhsvjzb.museums.cn

Zhù zhǐ: Shàn Jǐ Bīn Guǎngxī Zhuàngzú Zìzhìqū Hèzhōu Shì Zhāopíng Xiàn Shān Dé Lù 846 Hào Hèzōu Bó Wù Guǎn （Yóuzhèng Biānmǎ：721205）. Liánxì Diànhuà：44700076. Diànzǐ Yóuxiāng：vhslb@lmhsvjzb.museums.cn

Ji Bin Shan, Hezhou Museum, 846 Shan De Road, Zhaoping County, Hezhou, Guangxi Autonomous Region. Postal Code: 721205. Phone Number：44700076. E-mail：vhslb@lmhsvjzb.museums.cn

1365。姓名: 印刚兵

住址（寺庙）：广西壮族自治区钦州市钦北区庆铁路 540 号绅冠寺（邮政编码：480080）。联系电话：84213710。电子邮箱：sbzag@lkastfod.god.cn

Zhù zhǐ: Yìn Gāng Bīng Guǎngxī Zhuàngzú Zìzhìqū Qīnzhōu Shì Qīn Běi Qū Qìng Fū Lù 540 Hào Shēn Guān Sì （Yóuzhèng Biānmǎ：480080）. Liánxì Diànhuà：84213710. Diànzǐ Yóuxiāng：sbzag@lkastfod.god.cn

Gang Bing Yin, Shen Guan Temple, 540 Qing Fu Road, Qinbei District, Qinzhou, Guangxi Autonomous Region. Postal Code: 480080. Phone Number：84213710. E-mail：sbzag@lkastfod.god.cn

1366。姓名: 夹谷泽辙

住址（机场）：广西壮族自治区钦州市浦北县德寰路 858 号钦州谢陆国际机场（邮政编码：496779）。联系电话：58768359。电子邮箱：zwaqn@wmgxksad.airports.cn

Zhù zhǐ: Jiágǔ Zé Zhé Guǎngxī Zhuàngzú Zìzhìqū Qīnzhōu Shì Pǔ Běi Xiàn Dé Huán Lù 858 Hào Qīnzōu Xiè Liù Guó Jì Jī Chǎng （Yóuzhèng Biānmǎ：496779）. Liánxì Diànhuà：58768359. Diànzǐ Yóuxiāng：zwaqn@wmgxksad.airports.cn

Ze Zhe Jiagu, Qinzhou Xie Liu International Airport, 858 De Huan Road, Pubei County, Qinzhou, Guangxi Autonomous Region. Postal Code: 496779. Phone Number：58768359. E-mail：zwaqn@wmgxksad.airports.cn

1367。姓名: 车德龙

住址（公司）：广西壮族自治区贵港市覃塘区兵迅路 733 号愈独有限公司（邮政编码：485787）。联系电话：55536547。电子邮箱：tkjfb@auoxvnwp.biz.cn

Zhù zhǐ: Chē Dé Lóng Guǎngxī Zhuàngzú Zìzhìqū Guìgǎng Shì Tán Táng Qū Bīng Xùn Lù 733 Hào Yù Dú Yǒuxiàn Gōngsī (Yóuzhèng Biānmǎ：485787). Liánxì Diànhuà：55536547. Diànzǐ Yóuxiāng：tkjfb@auoxvnwp.biz.cn

De Long Che, Yu Du Corporation, 733 Bing Xun Road, Qintang District, Guigang, Guangxi Autonomous Region. Postal Code: 485787. Phone Number：55536547. E-mail：tkjfb@auoxvnwp.biz.cn

1368。姓名: 阴阳山

住址（公园）：广西壮族自治区来宾市忻城县白大路 927 号阳焯公园（邮政编码：734161）。联系电话：26816461。电子邮箱：quigb@ahksmewv.parks.cn

Zhù zhǐ: Yīn Yáng Shān Guǎngxī Zhuàngzú Zìzhìqū Láibīn Shì Xīn Chéng Xiàn Bái Dà Lù 927 Hào Yáng Chāo Gōng Yuán (Yóuzhèng Biānmǎ：734161). Liánxì Diànhuà：26816461. Diànzǐ Yóuxiāng：quigb@ahksmewv.parks.cn

Yang Shan Yin, Yang Chao Park, 927 Bai Da Road, Xincheng County, Laibin, Guangxi Autonomous Region. Postal Code: 734161. Phone Number：26816461. E-mail：quigb@ahksmewv.parks.cn

1369。姓名: 符盛食

住址（机场）：广西壮族自治区贺州市富川瑶族自治县豪源路 372 号贺州嘉翰国际机场（邮政编码：332752）。联系电话：50029130。电子邮箱：zbwft@zivngspf.airports.cn

Zhù zhǐ: Fú Chéng Sì Guǎngxī Zhuàngzú Zìzhìqū Hèzhōu Shì Fùchuān Yáozú Zìzhìxiàn Háo Yuán Lù 372 Hào Hèzōu Jiā Hàn Guó Jì Jī Chǎng（Yóuzhèng Biānmǎ：332752). Liánxì Diànhuà：50029130. Diànzǐ Yóuxiāng：zbwft@zivngspf.airports.cn

Cheng Si Fu, Hezhou Jia Han International Airport, 372 Hao Yuan Road, Fuchuan Yao Autonomous County, Hezhou, Guangxi Autonomous Region. Postal Code: 332752. Phone Number：50029130. E-mail：zbwft@zivngspf.airports.cn

1370。姓名: 师翼科

住址（湖泊）：广西壮族自治区玉林市北流市征葛路 550 号铁际湖（邮政编码：264746）。联系电话：96242781。电子邮箱：nkzgc@mwyqoctz.lakes.cn

Zhù zhǐ: Shī Yì Kē Guǎngxī Zhuàngzú Zìzhìqū Yùlín Shì Běi Liú Shì Zhēng Gé Lù 550 Hào Tiě Jì Hú（Yóuzhèng Biānmǎ：264746). Liánxì Diànhuà：96242781. Diànzǐ Yóuxiāng：nkzgc@mwyqoctz.lakes.cn

Yi Ke Shi, Tie Ji Lake, 550 Zheng Ge Road, Beiliu, Yulin, Guangxi Autonomous Region. Postal Code: 264746. Phone Number：96242781. E-mail：nkzgc@mwyqoctz.lakes.cn

1371。姓名: 尚珏译

住址（机场）：广西壮族自治区北海市合浦县澜炯路 806 号北海亚郁国际机场（邮政编码：795265）。联系电话：75586267。电子邮箱：gimlj@eosrymib.airports.cn

Zhù zhǐ: Shàng Jué Yì Guǎngxī Zhuàngzú Zìzhìqū Běihǎi Shì Hépǔ Xiàn Lán Jiǒng Lù 806 Hào Běiǎi Yà Yù Guó Jì Jī Chǎng（Yóuzhèng Biānmǎ：795265). Liánxì Diànhuà：75586267. Diànzǐ Yóuxiāng：gimlj@eosrymib.airports.cn

Jue Yi Shang, Beihai Ya Yu International Airport, 806 Lan Jiong Road, Hepu County, Beihai, Guangxi Autonomous Region. Postal Code: 795265. Phone Number：75586267. E-mail：gimlj@eosrymib.airports.cn

1372。姓名: 厍骥近

住址（公园）：广西壮族自治区柳州市柳城县盛际路 870 号敬不公园（邮政编码：662171）。联系电话：33708002。电子邮箱：cresp@glvmociu.parks.cn

Zhù zhǐ: Shè Jì Jìn Guǎngxī Zhuàngzú Zìzhìqū Liǔzhōu Shì Liǔchéng Xiàn Chéng Jì Lù 870 Hào Jìng Bù Gōng Yuán (Yóuzhèng Biānmǎ：662171). Liánxì Diànhuà：33708002. Diànzǐ Yóuxiāng：cresp@glvmociu.parks.cn

Ji Jin She, Jing Bu Park, 870 Cheng Ji Road, Liucheng County, Liuzhou, Guangxi Autonomous Region. Postal Code: 662171. Phone Number：33708002. E-mail：cresp@glvmociu.parks.cn

1373。姓名: 宦俊沛

住址（公司）：广西壮族自治区南宁市邕宁区光际路 329 号晗智有限公司（邮政编码：491839）。联系电话：71609258。电子邮箱：xrdpo@tjmqzvpy.biz.cn

Zhù zhǐ: Huàn Jùn Bèi Guǎngxī Zhuàngzú Zìzhìqū Nánníng Shì Yōng Níng Qū Guāng Jì Lù 329 Hào Hán Zhì Yǒuxiàn Gōngsī (Yóuzhèng Biānmǎ：491839). Liánxì Diànhuà：71609258. Diànzǐ Yóuxiāng：xrdpo@tjmqzvpy.biz.cn

Jun Bei Huan, Han Zhi Corporation, 329 Guang Ji Road, Yongning District, NanNing, Guangxi Autonomous Region. Postal Code: 491839. Phone Number：71609258. E-mail：xrdpo@tjmqzvpy.biz.cn

1374。姓名: 王寰渊

住址（广场）：广西壮族自治区南宁市宾阳县大进路 172 号亭斌广场（邮政编码：434692）。联系电话：86829689。电子邮箱：pbhrz@zqcplwja.squares.cn

Zhù zhǐ: Wáng Huán Yuān Guǎngxī Zhuàngzú Zìzhìqū Nánníng Shì Bīn Yáng Xiàn Dà Jìn Lù 172 Hào Tíng Bīn Guǎng Chǎng（Yóuzhèng Biānmǎ：434692). Liánxì Diànhuà：86829689. Diànzǐ Yóuxiāng：pbhrz@zqcplwja.squares.cn

Huan Yuan Wang, Ting Bin Square, 172 Da Jin Road, Binyang County, NanNing, Guangxi Autonomous Region. Postal Code: 434692. Phone Number：86829689. E-mail：pbhrz@zqcplwja.squares.cn

1375。姓名: 苍郁全

住址（湖泊）：广西壮族自治区梧州市蒙山县珂德路 835 号乐尚湖（邮政编码：931726）。联系电话：20102751。电子邮箱：iwrvx@quglxyeo.lakes.cn

Zhù zhǐ: Cāng Yù Quán Guǎngxī Zhuàngzú Zìzhìqū Wúzhōu Shì Méng Shānxiàn Kē Dé Lù 835 Hào Lè Shàng Hú（Yóuzhèng Biānmǎ：931726). Liánxì Diànhuà：20102751. Diànzǐ Yóuxiāng：iwrvx@quglxyeo.lakes.cn

Yu Quan Cang, Le Shang Lake, 835 Ke De Road, Mengshan County, Wuzhou, Guangxi Autonomous Region. Postal Code: 931726. Phone Number：20102751. E-mail：iwrvx@quglxyeo.lakes.cn

1376。姓名: 呼延中舟

住址（医院）：广西壮族自治区崇左市宁明县愈仲路 696 号钦兵医院（邮政编码：526688）。联系电话：57094920。电子邮箱：kurje@uwjiaztq.health.cn

Zhù zhǐ: Hūyán Zhōng Zhōu Guǎngxī Zhuàngzú Zìzhìqū Chóng Zuǒ Shì Níng Míng Xiàn Yù Zhòng Lù 696 Hào Qīn Bīng Yī Yuàn（Yóuzhèng Biānmǎ：526688). Liánxì Diànhuà：57094920. Diànzǐ Yóuxiāng：kurje@uwjiaztq.health.cn

Zhong Zhou Huyan, Qin Bing Hospital, 696 Yu Zhong Road, Ningming County, Chongzuo, Guangxi Autonomous Region. Postal Code: 526688. Phone Number：57094920. E-mail：kurje@uwjiaztq.health.cn

1377。姓名: 裘轶南

住址（博物院）：广西壮族自治区桂林市叠彩区绅珂路 161 号桂林博物馆（邮政编码：756573）。联系电话：95536203。电子邮箱：rypdl@geowhlan.museums.cn

Zhù zhǐ: Qiú Yì Nán Guǎngxī Zhuàngzú Zìzhìqū Guìlín Shì Dié Cǎi Qū Shēn Kē Lù 161 Hào Gulín Bó Wù Guǎn (Yóuzhèng Biānmǎ：756573). Liánxì Diànhuà：95536203. Diànzǐ Yóuxiāng：rypdl@geowhlan.museums.cn

Yi Nan Qiu, Guilin Museum, 161 Shen Ke Road, Folding Area, Guilin, Guangxi Autonomous Region. Postal Code: 756573. Phone Number：95536203. E-mail：rypdl@geowhlan.museums.cn

1378。姓名: 寿启不

住址（家庭）：广西壮族自治区防城港市东兴市宽恩路 975 号己锤公寓 17 层 321 室（邮政编码：744380）。联系电话：47523432。电子邮箱：coeus@ytfojeqi.cn

Zhù zhǐ: Shòu Qǐ Bù Guǎngxī Zhuàngzú Zìzhìqū Fángchénggǎng Shì Dōng Xīng Shì Kuān Ēn Lù 975 Hào Jǐ Chuí Gōng Yù 17 Céng 321 Shì (Yóuzhèng Biānmǎ：744380). Liánxì Diànhuà：47523432. Diànzǐ Yóuxiāng：coeus@ytfojeqi.cn

Qi Bu Shou, Room# 321, Floor# 17, Ji Chui Apartment, 975 Kuan En Road, Dongxing City, Fangchenggang, Guangxi Autonomous Region. Postal Code: 744380. Phone Number：47523432. E-mail：coeus@ytfojeqi.cn

1379。姓名: 从愈昌

住址（火车站）：广西壮族自治区北海市铁山港区人绅路 962 号北海站（邮政编码：313121）。联系电话：79296854。电子邮箱：qzogl@bdrwpnft.chr.cn

Zhù zhǐ: Cóng Yù Chāng Guǎngxī Zhuàngzú Zìzhìqū Běihǎi Shì Tiě Shān Gǎng Qū Rén Shēn Lù 962 Hào Běiǎi Zhàn（Yóuzhèng Biānmǎ：313121）. Liánxì Diànhuà：79296854. Diànzǐ Yóuxiāng：qzogl@bdrwpnft.chr.cn

Yu Chang Cong, Beihai Railway Station, 962 Ren Shen Road, Iron Mountain Port District, Beihai, Guangxi Autonomous Region. Postal Code: 313121. Phone Number：79296854. E-mail：qzogl@bdrwpnft.chr.cn

1380。姓名: 申冠超

住址（博物院）：广西壮族自治区崇左市宁明县翰友路 570 号崇左博物馆（邮政编码：537619）。联系电话：32290427。电子邮箱：ztjwo@vezahwqr.museums.cn

Zhù zhǐ: Shēn Guàn Chāo Guǎngxī Zhuàngzú Zìzhìqū Chóng Zuǒ Shì Níng Míng Xiàn Hàn Yǒu Lù 570 Hào Cóng Zuǒ Bó Wù Guǎn（Yóuzhèng Biānmǎ：537619）. Liánxì Diànhuà：32290427. Diànzǐ Yóuxiāng：ztjwo@vezahwqr.museums.cn

Guan Chao Shen, Chongzuo Museum, 570 Han You Road, Ningming County, Chongzuo, Guangxi Autonomous Region. Postal Code: 537619. Phone Number：32290427. E-mail：ztjwo@vezahwqr.museums.cn

1381。姓名: 劳炯山

住址（寺庙）：广西壮族自治区贺州市昭平县澜原路 703 号沛岐寺（邮政编码：464851）。联系电话：52437090。电子邮箱：vngps@fiojzcqm.god.cn

Zhù zhǐ: Láo Jiǒng Shān Guǎngxī Zhuàngzú Zìzhìqū Hèzhōu Shì Zhāopíng Xiàn Lán Yuán Lù 703 Hào Bèi Qí Sì (Yóuzhèng Biānmǎ：464851). Liánxì Diànhuà：52437090. Diànzǐ Yóuxiāng：vngps@fiojzcqm.god.cn

Jiong Shan Lao, Bei Qi Temple, 703 Lan Yuan Road, Zhaoping County, Hezhou, Guangxi Autonomous Region. Postal Code: 464851. Phone Number：52437090. E-mail：vngps@fiojzcqm.god.cn

1382。姓名: 查仓甫

住址（火车站）：广西壮族自治区柳州市柳北区超金路 326 号柳州站（邮政编码：401143）。联系电话：89223776。电子邮箱：tupbm@olzuyitp.chr.cn

Zhù zhǐ: Zhā Cāng Fǔ Guǎngxī Zhuàngzú Zìzhìqū Liǔzhōu Shì Liǔběi Qū Chāo Jīn Lù 326 Hào Liǔzōu Zhàn (Yóuzhèng Biānmǎ：401143). Liánxì Diànhuà：89223776. Diànzǐ Yóuxiāng：tupbm@olzuyitp.chr.cn

Cang Fu Zha, Liuzhou Railway Station, 326 Chao Jin Road, Liubei District, Liuzhou, Guangxi Autonomous Region. Postal Code: 401143. Phone Number：89223776. E-mail：tupbm@olzuyitp.chr.cn

1383。姓名: 袁大臻

住址（公司）：广西壮族自治区来宾市象州县阳大路 447 号勇翰有限公司（邮政编码：974699）。联系电话：59500156。电子邮箱：guxlo@faqwxspg.biz.cn

Zhù zhǐ: Yuán Dài Zhēn Guǎngxī Zhuàngzú Zìzhìqū Láibīn Shì Xiàng Zhōu Xiàn Yáng Dà Lù 447 Hào Yǒng Hàn Yǒuxiàn Gōngsī (Yóuzhèng Biānmǎ：974699). Liánxì Diànhuà：59500156. Diànzǐ Yóuxiāng：guxlo@faqwxspg.biz.cn

Dai Zhen Yuan, Yong Han Corporation, 447 Yang Da Road, Xiangzhou County, Laibin, Guangxi Autonomous Region. Postal Code: 974699. Phone Number：59500156. E-mail：guxlo@faqwxspg.biz.cn

1384。姓名: 计克进

住址（广场）：广西壮族自治区柳州市城中区金员路 747 号圣波广场（邮政编码：419756）。联系电话：19676090。电子邮箱：kuotz@ngwsxrfu.squares.cn

Zhù zhǐ: Jì Kè Jìn Guǎngxī Zhuàngzú Zìzhìqū Liǔzhōu Shì Chéngzhōng Qū Jīn Yuán Lù 747 Hào Shèng Bō Guǎng Chǎng (Yóuzhèng Biānmǎ：419756). Liánxì Diànhuà：19676090. Diànzǐ Yóuxiāng：kuotz@ngwsxrfu.squares.cn

Ke Jin Ji, Sheng Bo Square, 747 Jin Yuan Road, Chengzhong District, Liuzhou, Guangxi Autonomous Region. Postal Code: 419756. Phone Number：19676090. E-mail：kuotz@ngwsxrfu.squares.cn

1385。姓名: 暨鹤民

住址（大学）：广西壮族自治区贵港市港北区红圣大学游仓路 162 号（邮政编码：238408）。联系电话：74490528。电子邮箱：zelqd@xhntsukq.edu.cn

Zhù zhǐ: Jì Hè Mín Guǎngxī Zhuàngzú Zìzhìqū Guìgǎng Shì Gǎngběi Qū Hóng Shèng DàxuéYóu Cāng Lù 162 Hào (Yóuzhèng Biānmǎ：238408). Liánxì Diànhuà：74490528. Diànzǐ Yóuxiāng：zelqd@xhntsukq.edu.cn

He Min Ji, Hong Sheng University, 162 You Cang Road, Gangbei District, Guigang, Guangxi Autonomous Region. Postal Code: 238408. Phone Number：74490528. E-mail：zelqd@xhntsukq.edu.cn

1386。姓名: 况福王

住址（机场）：广西壮族自治区防城港市上思县汉迅路 740 号防城港尚锤国际机场（邮政编码：114080）。联系电话：51236178。电子邮箱：qjazo@hmxwfiaz.airports.cn

Zhù zhǐ: Kuàng Fú Wáng Guǎngxī Zhuàngzú Zìzhìqū Fángchénggǎng Shì Shàng Sī Xiàn Hàn Xùn Lù 740 Hào Fángcénggǎng Shàng Chuí Guó Jì Jī Chǎng （Yóuzhèng Biānmǎ：114080). Liánxì Diànhuà：51236178. Diànzǐ Yóuxiāng：qjazo@hmxwfiaz.airports.cn

Fu Wang Kuang, Fangchenggang Shang Chui International Airport, 740 Han Xun Road, Shangsi County, Fangchenggang, Guangxi Autonomous Region. Postal Code: 114080. Phone Number：51236178. E-mail：qjazo@hmxwfiaz.airports.cn

1387。姓名: 蓟国进

住址（医院）：广西壮族自治区钦州市灵山县己稼路 786 号沛臻医院（邮政编码：187062）。联系电话：60367103。电子邮箱：xkwpo@midrqwtb.health.cn

Zhù zhǐ: Jì Guó Jìn Guǎngxī Zhuàngzú Zìzhìqū Qīnzhōu Shì Língshān Xiàn Jǐ Jià Lù 786 Hào Bèi Zhēn Yī Yuàn （Yóuzhèng Biānmǎ：187062). Liánxì Diànhuà：60367103. Diànzǐ Yóuxiāng：xkwpo@midrqwtb.health.cn

Guo Jin Ji, Bei Zhen Hospital, 786 Ji Jia Road, Lingshan County, Qinzhou, Guangxi Autonomous Region. Postal Code: 187062. Phone Number：60367103. E-mail：xkwpo@midrqwtb.health.cn

1388。姓名: 太叔守豪

住址（机场）：广西壮族自治区百色市靖西市辉福路 884 号百色独维国际机场（邮政编码：148920）。联系电话：88936402。电子邮箱：fnmhg@yvcnhqwu.airports.cn

Zhù zhǐ: Tàishū Shǒu Háo Guǎngxī Zhuàngzú Zìzhìqū Bǎisè Shì Jìng Xī Shì Huī Fú Lù 884 Hào Bǎisè Dú Wéi Guó Jì Jī Chǎng（Yóuzhèng Biānmǎ：148920）. Liánxì Diànhuà：88936402. Diànzǐ Yóuxiāng：fnmhg@yvcnhqwu.airports.cn

Shou Hao Taishu, Baise Du Wei International Airport, 884 Hui Fu Road, Jingxi, Baise, Guangxi Autonomous Region. Postal Code: 148920. Phone Number：88936402. E-mail：fnmhg@yvcnhqwu.airports.cn

1389。姓名: 况光智

住址（大学）：广西壮族自治区防城港市上思县澜舟大学屹焯路 889 号（邮政编码：448866）。联系电话：20475763。电子邮箱：bqomj@oxunwyek.edu.cn

Zhù zhǐ: Kuàng Guāng Zhì Guǎngxī Zhuàngzú Zìzhìqū Fángchénggǎng Shì Shàng Sī Xiàn Lán Zhōu Dàxué Yì Chāo Lù 889 Hào（Yóuzhèng Biānmǎ：448866）. Liánxì Diànhuà：20475763. Diànzǐ Yóuxiāng：bqomj@oxunwyek.edu.cn

Guang Zhi Kuang, Lan Zhou University, 889 Yi Chao Road, Shangsi County, Fangchenggang, Guangxi Autonomous Region. Postal Code: 448866. Phone Number：20475763. E-mail：bqomj@oxunwyek.edu.cn

1390。姓名: 南门亮晗

住址（医院）：广西壮族自治区贺州市昭平县国祥路 195 号红豪医院（邮政编码：464794）。联系电话：30639230。电子邮箱：qyohv@bxfwtnzu.health.cn

Zhù zhǐ: Nánmén Liàng Hán Guǎngxī Zhuàngzú Zìzhìqū Hèzhōu Shì Zhāopíng Xiàn Guó Xiáng Lù 195 Hào Hóng Háo Yī Yuàn（Yóuzhèng Biānmǎ：464794）. Liánxì Diànhuà：30639230. Diànzǐ Yóuxiāng：qyohv@bxfwtnzu.health.cn

Liang Han Nanmen, Hong Hao Hospital, 195 Guo Xiang Road, Zhaoping County, Hezhou, Guangxi Autonomous Region. Postal Code: 464794. Phone Number：30639230. E-mail：qyohv@bxfwtnzu.health.cn

1391。姓名：茅仓际

住址（医院）：广西壮族自治区崇左市天等县柱寰路 539 号隆稼医院（邮政编码：349881）。联系电话：80727832。电子邮箱：sqiux@fzxvtcjm.health.cn

Zhù zhǐ: Máo Cāng Jì Guǎngxī Zhuàngzú Zìzhìqū Chóng Zuǒ Shì Tiān Děng Xiàn Zhù Huán Lù 539 Hào Lóng Jià Yī Yuàn（Yóuzhèng Biānmǎ：349881). Liánxì Diànhuà：80727832. Diànzǐ Yóuxiāng：sqiux@fzxvtcjm.health.cn

Cang Ji Mao, Long Jia Hospital, 539 Zhu Huan Road, Tiandeng County, Chongzuo, Guangxi Autonomous Region. Postal Code: 349881. Phone Number：80727832. E-mail：sqiux@fzxvtcjm.health.cn

1392。姓名：毂梁石宝

住址（大学）：广西壮族自治区北海市铁山港区彬中大学勇强路 271 号（邮政编码：621626）。联系电话：83674077。电子邮箱：qtouv@befcwpjk.edu.cn

Zhù zhǐ: Gǔliáng Shí Bǎo Guǎngxī Zhuàngzú Zìzhìqū Běihǎi Shì Tiě Shān Gǎng Qū Bīn Zhōng Dàxué Yǒng Qiǎng Lù 271 Hào（Yóuzhèng Biānmǎ：621626). Liánxì Diànhuà：83674077. Diànzǐ Yóuxiāng：qtouv@befcwpjk.edu.cn

Shi Bao Guliang, Bin Zhong University, 271 Yong Qiang Road, Iron Mountain Port District, Beihai, Guangxi Autonomous Region. Postal Code: 621626. Phone Number：83674077. E-mail：qtouv@befcwpjk.edu.cn

1393。姓名：全茂居

住址（公园）：广西壮族自治区桂林市兴安县立员路 596 号红石公园（邮政编码：415274）。联系电话：66738583。电子邮箱：itkhz@berzsivg.parks.cn

Zhù zhǐ: Quán Mào Jū Guǎngxī Zhuàngzú Zìzhìqū Guìlín Shì Xìngān Xiàn Lì Yuán Lù 596 Hào Hóng Dàn Gōng Yuán（Yóuzhèng Biānmǎ：415274). Liánxì Diànhuà：66738583. Diànzǐ Yóuxiāng：itkhz@berzsivg.parks.cn

Mao Ju Quan, Hong Dan Park, 596 Li Yuan Road, Xingan County, Guilin, Guangxi Autonomous Region. Postal Code: 415274. Phone Number：66738583. E-mail：itkhz@berzsivg.parks.cn

1394。姓名: 荣德冠

住址（湖泊）：广西壮族自治区百色市右江区南土路 593 号焯寰湖（邮政编码：602084）。联系电话：83781101。电子邮箱：coivq@fpmdbrnh.lakes.cn

Zhù zhǐ: Róng Dé Guān Guǎngxī Zhuàngzú Zìzhìqū Bǎisè Shì Yòu Jiāng Qū Nán Tǔ Lù 593 Hào Zhuō Huán Hú（Yóuzhèng Biānmǎ：602084）. Liánxì Diànhuà: 83781101. Diànzǐ Yóuxiāng：coivq@fpmdbrnh.lakes.cn

De Guan Rong, Zhuo Huan Lake, 593 Nan Tu Road, Youjiang District, Baise, Guangxi Autonomous Region. Postal Code: 602084. Phone Number：83781101. E-mail：coivq@fpmdbrnh.lakes.cn

1395。姓名: 乜启立

住址（博物院）：广西壮族自治区来宾市忻城县祥水路 929 号来宾博物馆（邮政编码：971680）。联系电话：51021909。电子邮箱：nrfbz@lfrocade.museums.cn

Zhù zhǐ: Niè Qǐ Lì Guǎngxī Zhuàngzú Zìzhìqū Láibīn Shì Xīn Chéng Xiàn Xiáng Shuǐ Lù 929 Hào Láibīn Bó Wù Guǎn（Yóuzhèng Biānmǎ：971680）. Liánxì Diànhuà: 51021909. Diànzǐ Yóuxiāng：nrfbz@lfrocade.museums.cn

Qi Li Nie, Laibin Museum, 929 Xiang Shui Road, Xincheng County, Laibin, Guangxi Autonomous Region. Postal Code: 971680. Phone Number：51021909. E-mail：nrfbz@lfrocade.museums.cn

1396。姓名: 微先王

住址（寺庙）：广西壮族自治区玉林市陆川县队锤路 134 号陆恩寺（邮政编码：382860）。联系电话：73088031。电子邮箱：unbsz@feghkymr.god.cn

Zhù zhǐ: Wēi Xiān Wàng Guǎngxī Zhuàngzú Zìzhìqū Yùlín Shì Lù Chuān Xiàn Duì Chuí Lù 134 Hào Lù Ēn Sì (Yóuzhèng Biānmǎ： 382860). Liánxì Diànhuà： 73088031. Diànzǐ Yóuxiāng： unbsz@feghkymr.god.cn

Xian Wang Wei, Lu En Temple, 134 Dui Chui Road, Luchuan County, Yulin, Guangxi Autonomous Region. Postal Code: 382860. Phone Number： 73088031. E-mail： unbsz@feghkymr.god.cn

1397。姓名: 甄大稼

住址（公园）：广西壮族自治区百色市乐业县大兵路 906 号全俊公园（邮政编码：361957）。联系电话：38307130。电子邮箱：
ebixo@nurwzahq.parks.cn

Zhù zhǐ: Zhēn Dà Jià Guǎngxī Zhuàngzú Zìzhìqū Bǎisè Shì Lè Yè Xiàn Dài Bīng Lù 906 Hào Quán Jùn Gōng Yuán (Yóuzhèng Biānmǎ： 361957). Liánxì Diànhuà： 38307130. Diànzǐ Yóuxiāng： ebixo@nurwzahq.parks.cn

Da Jia Zhen, Quan Jun Park, 906 Dai Bing Road, Leye County, Baise, Guangxi Autonomous Region. Postal Code: 361957. Phone Number： 38307130. E-mail： ebixo@nurwzahq.parks.cn

1398。姓名: 郗斌成

住址（博物院）：广西壮族自治区桂林市灌阳县铁不路 468 号桂林博物馆（邮政编码：886769）。联系电话：18087695。电子邮箱：
kixqt@xadopibg.museums.cn

Zhù zhǐ: Xī Bīn Chéng Guǎngxī Zhuàngzú Zìzhìqū Guìlín Shì Guàn Yáng Xiàn Fū Bù Lù 468 Hào Gulín Bó Wù Guǎn (Yóuzhèng Biānmǎ： 886769). Liánxì Diànhuà： 18087695. Diànzǐ Yóuxiāng： kixqt@xadopibg.museums.cn

Bin Cheng Xi, Guilin Museum, 468 Fu Bu Road, Guanyang County, Guilin, Guangxi Autonomous Region. Postal Code: 886769. Phone Number： 18087695. E-mail： kixqt@xadopibg.museums.cn

1399。姓名:越铁晗

住址（大学）：广西壮族自治区钦州市浦北县石冠大学可骥路 977 号（邮政编码：750231）。联系电话：27128875。电子邮箱：tkbzs@edjhougm.edu.cn

Zhù zhǐ: Yuè Fū Hán Guǎngxī Zhuàngzú Zìzhìqū Qīnzhōu Shì Pǔ Běi Xiàn Dàn Guān DàxuéKě Jì Lù 977 Hào （Yóuzhèng Biānmǎ：750231). Liánxì Diànhuà：27128875. Diànzǐ Yóuxiāng：tkbzs@edjhougm.edu.cn

Fu Han Yue, Dan Guan University, 977 Ke Ji Road, Pubei County, Qinzhou, Guangxi Autonomous Region. Postal Code: 750231. Phone Number：27128875. E-mail：tkbzs@edjhougm.edu.cn

1400。姓名:仲孙茂甫

住址（湖泊）：广西壮族自治区贺州市昭平县王帆路 488 号石奎湖（邮政编码：454358）。联系电话：28547340。电子邮箱：mubis@gdphaqyl.lakes.cn

Zhù zhǐ: Zhòngsūn Mào Fǔ Guǎngxī Zhuàngzú Zìzhìqū Hèzhōu Shì Zhāopíng Xiàn Wáng Fān Lù 488 Hào Dàn Kuí Hú （Yóuzhèng Biānmǎ：454358). Liánxì Diànhuà：28547340. Diànzǐ Yóuxiāng：mubis@gdphaqyl.lakes.cn

Mao Fu Zhongsun, Dan Kui Lake, 488 Wang Fan Road, Zhaoping County, Hezhou, Guangxi Autonomous Region. Postal Code: 454358. Phone Number：28547340. E-mail：mubis@gdphaqyl.lakes.cn

1401。姓名:况先彬

住址（公共汽车站）：广西壮族自治区桂林市临桂区友先路 221 号勇寰站（邮政编码：505076）。联系电话：72596703。电子邮箱：eymaj@tcybuwxi.transport.cn

Zhù zhǐ: Kuàng Xiān Bīn Guǎngxī Zhuàngzú Zìzhìqū Guìlín Shì Lín Guì Qū Yǒu Xiān Lù 221 Hào Yǒng Huán Zhàn （Yóuzhèng Biānmǎ：505076). Liánxì Diànhuà：72596703. Diànzǐ Yóuxiāng：eymaj@tcybuwxi.transport.cn

Xian Bin Kuang, Yong Huan Bus Station, 221 You Xian Road, Lingui District, Guilin, Guangxi Autonomous Region. Postal Code: 505076. Phone Number：72596703. E-mail：eymaj@tcybuwxi.transport.cn

1402。姓名: 项福钦

住址（机场）：广西壮族自治区来宾市合山市己尚路 408 号来宾乐石国际机场（邮政编码：985755）。联系电话：98750717。电子邮箱：zwtod@akevloqm.airports.cn

Zhù zhǐ: Xiàng Fú Qīn Guǎngxī Zhuàngzú Zìzhìqū Láibīn Shì Hé Shān Shì Jǐ Shàng Lù 408 Hào Láibīn Lè Dàn Guó Jì Jī Chǎng（Yóuzhèng Biānmǎ：985755). Liánxì Diànhuà：98750717. Diànzǐ Yóuxiāng：zwtod@akevloqm.airports.cn

Fu Qin Xiang, Laibin Le Dan International Airport, 408 Ji Shang Road, Heshan City, Laibin, Guangxi Autonomous Region. Postal Code: 985755. Phone Number：98750717. E-mail：zwtod@akevloqm.airports.cn

1403。姓名: 宦圣进

住址（酒店）：广西壮族自治区玉林市兴业县征南路 373 号宽坡酒店（邮政编码：287273）。联系电话：85023262。电子邮箱：wozdp@zslivcdq.biz.cn

Zhù zhǐ: Huàn Shèng Jìn Guǎngxī Zhuàngzú Zìzhìqū Yùlín Shì Xìngyè Xiàn Zhēng Nán Lù 373 Hào Kuān Pō Jiǔ Diàn（Yóuzhèng Biānmǎ：287273). Liánxì Diànhuà：85023262. Diànzǐ Yóuxiāng：wozdp@zslivcdq.biz.cn

Sheng Jin Huan, Kuan Po Hotel, 373 Zheng Nan Road, Xingye County, Yulin, Guangxi Autonomous Region. Postal Code: 287273. Phone Number：85023262. E-mail：wozdp@zslivcdq.biz.cn

1404。姓名: 瞿奎迅

住址（大学）：广西壮族自治区梧州市龙圩区熔宝大学振陆路 573 号（邮政编码：552221）。联系电话：11331202。电子邮箱：ibkda@plwkxces.edu.cn

Zhù zhǐ: Qú Kuí Xùn Guǎngxī Zhuàngzú Zìzhìqū Wúzhōu Shì Lóng Wéi Qū Róng Bǎo DàxuéZhèn Liù Lù 573 Hào（Yóuzhèng Biānmǎ：552221). Liánxì Diànhuà：11331202. Diànzǐ Yóuxiāng：ibkda@plwkxces.edu.cn

Kui Xun Qu, Rong Bao University, 573 Zhen Liu Road, Longxu District, Wuzhou, Guangxi Autonomous Region. Postal Code: 552221. Phone Number：11331202. E-mail：ibkda@plwkxces.edu.cn

1405。姓名: 陶中澜

住址（寺庙）：广西壮族自治区来宾市合山市桥坚路 262 号居金寺（邮政编码：586568）。联系电话：32526338。电子邮箱：nrftk@jyhdqnok.god.cn

Zhù zhǐ: Táo Zhòng Lán Guǎngxī Zhuàngzú Zìzhìqū Láibīn Shì Hé Shān Shì Qiáo Jiān Lù 262 Hào Jū Jīn Sì（Yóuzhèng Biānmǎ：586568). Liánxì Diànhuà：32526338. Diànzǐ Yóuxiāng：nrftk@jyhdqnok.god.cn

Zhong Lan Tao, Ju Jin Temple, 262 Qiao Jian Road, Heshan City, Laibin, Guangxi Autonomous Region. Postal Code: 586568. Phone Number：32526338. E-mail：nrftk@jyhdqnok.god.cn

1406。姓名: 陈民石

住址（博物院）：广西壮族自治区贺州市富川瑶族自治县柱南路 651 号贺州博物馆（邮政编码：986601）。联系电话：30440020。电子邮箱：kdmsh@owejbyku.museums.cn

Zhù zhǐ: Chén Mín Dàn Guǎngxī Zhuàngzú Zìzhìqū Hèzhōu Shì Fùchuān Yáozú Zìzhìxiàn Zhù Nán Lù 651 Hào Hèzōu Bó Wù Guǎn（Yóuzhèng Biānmǎ：986601). Liánxì Diànhuà：30440020. Diànzǐ Yóuxiāng：kdmsh@owejbyku.museums.cn

Min Dan Chen, Hezhou Museum, 651 Zhu Nan Road, Fuchuan Yao Autonomous County, Hezhou, Guangxi Autonomous Region. Postal Code: 986601. Phone Number：30440020. E-mail：kdmsh@owejbyku.museums.cn

1407。姓名: 祁熔晗

住址（广场）：广西壮族自治区玉林市玉州区泽铭路 819 号伦洵广场（邮政编码：868061）。联系电话：17195813。电子邮箱：mxiqe@bwztuoex.squares.cn

Zhù zhǐ: Qí Róng Hán Guǎngxī Zhuàngzú Zìzhìqū Yùlín Shì Yù Zhōu Qū Zé Míng Lù 819 Hào Lún Xún Guǎng Chǎng（Yóuzhèng Biānmǎ：868061）. Liánxì Diànhuà：17195813. Diànzǐ Yóuxiāng：mxiqe@bwztuoex.squares.cn

Rong Han Qi, Lun Xun Square, 819 Ze Ming Road, Yuzhou District, Yulin, Guangxi Autonomous Region. Postal Code: 868061. Phone Number：17195813. E-mail：mxiqe@bwztuoex.squares.cn

1408。姓名: 闻禹珂

住址（湖泊）：广西壮族自治区钦州市浦北县可员路 175 号俊白湖（邮政编码：469988）。联系电话：22541948。电子邮箱：pgcoq@pnumfyjv.lakes.cn

Zhù zhǐ: Wén Yǔ Kē Guǎngxī Zhuàngzú Zìzhìqū Qīnzhōu Shì Pǔ Běi Xiàn Kě Yuán Lù 175 Hào Jùn Bái Hú（Yóuzhèng Biānmǎ：469988）. Liánxì Diànhuà：22541948. Diànzǐ Yóuxiāng：pgcoq@pnumfyjv.lakes.cn

Yu Ke Wen, Jun Bai Lake, 175 Ke Yuan Road, Pubei County, Qinzhou, Guangxi Autonomous Region. Postal Code: 469988. Phone Number：22541948. E-mail：pgcoq@pnumfyjv.lakes.cn

1409。姓名: 宗学锤

住址（寺庙）：广西壮族自治区河池市天峨县屹南路 926 号阳鹤寺（邮政编码：586565）。联系电话：48552563。电子邮箱：dwbij@rqjhmgty.god.cn

Zhù zhǐ: Zōng Xué Chuí Guǎngxī Zhuàngzú Zìzhìqū Héchí Shì Tiān É Xiàn Yì Nán Lù 926 Hào Yáng Hè Sì（Yóuzhèng Biānmǎ：586565）. Liánxì Diànhuà：48552563. Diànzǐ Yóuxiāng：dwbij@rqjhmgty.god.cn

Xue Chui Zong, Yang He Temple, 926 Yi Nan Road, Tiane County, Hechi, Guangxi Autonomous Region. Postal Code: 586565. Phone Number：48552563. E-mail：dwbij@rqjhmgty.god.cn

1410。姓名: 袁威屹

住址（火车站）：广西壮族自治区河池市宜州区铭民路 621 号河池站（邮政编码：517539）。联系电话：96727771。电子邮箱：dgplv@nwfopqeb.chr.cn

Zhù zhǐ: Yuán Wēi Yì Guǎngxī Zhuàngzú Zìzhìqū Héchí Shì Yí zhōu qū Míng Mín Lù 621 Hào Hécí Zhàn（Yóuzhèng Biānmǎ：517539). Liánxì Diànhuà：96727771. Diànzǐ Yóuxiāng：dgplv@nwfopqeb.chr.cn

Wei Yi Yuan, Hechi Railway Station, 621 Ming Min Road, Yizhou District, Hechi, Guangxi Autonomous Region. Postal Code: 517539. Phone Number：96727771. E-mail：dgplv@nwfopqeb.chr.cn

CHAPTER 3: NAME, SURNAME & ADDRESSES (61-90)

1411。姓名: 段干辙成

住址（酒店）：广西壮族自治区钦州市钦北区际来路 132 号食学酒店（邮政编码：784094）。联系电话：14122136。电子邮箱：hizlx@mtcqrbyo.biz.cn

Zhù zhǐ: Duàngān Zhé Chéng Guǎngxī Zhuàngzú Zìzhìqū Qīnzhōu Shì Qīn Běi Qū Jì Lái Lù 132 Hào Yì Xué Jiǔ Diàn (Yóuzhèng Biānmǎ：784094). Liánxì Diànhuà：14122136. Diànzǐ Yóuxiāng：hizlx@mtcqrbyo.biz.cn

Zhe Cheng Duangan, Yi Xue Hotel, 132 Ji Lai Road, Qinbei District, Qinzhou, Guangxi Autonomous Region. Postal Code: 784094. Phone Number：14122136. E-mail：hizlx@mtcqrbyo.biz.cn

1412。姓名: 计亭甫

住址（机场）：广西壮族自治区贺州市富川瑶族自治县嘉勇路 809 号贺州学波国际机场（邮政编码：200610）。联系电话：84977452。电子邮箱：fyugz@gvodmefh.airports.cn

Zhù zhǐ: Jì Tíng Fǔ Guǎngxī Zhuàngzú Zìzhìqū Hèzhōu Shì Fùchuān Yáozú Zìzhìxiàn Jiā Yǒng Lù 809 Hào Hèzōu Xué Bō Guó Jì Jī Chǎng (Yóuzhèng Biānmǎ：200610). Liánxì Diànhuà：84977452. Diànzǐ Yóuxiāng：fyugz@gvodmefh.airports.cn

Ting Fu Ji, Hezhou Xue Bo International Airport, 809 Jia Yong Road, Fuchuan Yao Autonomous County, Hezhou, Guangxi Autonomous Region. Postal Code: 200610. Phone Number：84977452. E-mail：fyugz@gvodmefh.airports.cn

1413。姓名: 宁圣兵

住址（医院）：广西壮族自治区桂林市灵川县队钦路 154 号翰继医院（邮政编码：593212）。联系电话：16704222。电子邮箱：nmhui@osmpdtuj.health.cn

Zhù zhǐ: Nìng Shèng Bīng Guǎngxī Zhuàngzú Zìzhìqū Guìlín Shì Líng Chuānxiàn Duì Qīn Lù 154 Hào Hàn Jì Yī Yuàn (Yóuzhèng Biānmǎ：593212). Liánxì Diànhuà：16704222. Diànzǐ Yóuxiāng：nmhui@osmpdtuj.health.cn

Sheng Bing Ning, Han Ji Hospital, 154 Dui Qin Road, Lingchuan County, Guilin, Guangxi Autonomous Region. Postal Code: 593212. Phone Number：16704222. E-mail：nmhui@osmpdtuj.health.cn

1414。姓名: 蓝沛居

住址（酒店）：广西壮族自治区河池市宜州区谢惟路 352 号超秀酒店（邮政编码：961295）。联系电话：29869659。电子邮箱：fcwgh@ejcdlvoi.biz.cn

Zhù zhǐ: Lán Bèi Jū Guǎngxī Zhuàngzú Zìzhìqū Héchí Shì Yí zhōu qū Xiè Wéi Lù 352 Hào Chāo Xiù Jiǔ Diàn (Yóuzhèng Biānmǎ：961295). Liánxì Diànhuà：29869659. Diànzǐ Yóuxiāng：fcwgh@ejcdlvoi.biz.cn

Bei Ju Lan, Chao Xiu Hotel, 352 Xie Wei Road, Yizhou District, Hechi, Guangxi Autonomous Region. Postal Code: 961295. Phone Number：29869659. E-mail：fcwgh@ejcdlvoi.biz.cn

1415。姓名: 尤振进

住址（公共汽车站）：广西壮族自治区桂林市灌阳县威发路 571 号国翼站（邮政编码：608395）。联系电话：86020939。电子邮箱：fdgwe@wfsqizke.transport.cn

Zhù zhǐ: Yóu Zhèn Jìn Guǎngxī Zhuàngzú Zìzhìqū Guìlín Shì Guàn Yáng Xiàn Wēi Fā Lù 571 Hào Guó Yì Zhàn (Yóuzhèng Biānmǎ：608395). Liánxì Diànhuà：86020939. Diànzǐ Yóuxiāng：fdgwe@wfsqizke.transport.cn

Zhen Jin You, Guo Yi Bus Station, 571 Wei Fa Road, Guanyang County, Guilin, Guangxi Autonomous Region. Postal Code: 608395. Phone Number：86020939. E-mail：fdgwe@wfsqizke.transport.cn

1416。姓名: 佘铭钦

住址（公园）：广西壮族自治区崇左市天等县斌阳路 277 号坡宝公园（邮政编码：316061）。联系电话：11859821。电子邮箱：edqfr@sqczebto.parks.cn

Zhù zhǐ: Shé Míng Qīn Guǎngxī Zhuàngzú Zìzhìqū Chóng Zuǒ Shì Tiān Děng Xiàn Bīn Yáng Lù 277 Hào Pō Bǎo Gōng Yuán（Yóuzhèng Biānmǎ：316061）. Liánxì Diànhuà：11859821. Diànzǐ Yóuxiāng： edqfr@sqczebto.parks.cn

Ming Qin She, Po Bao Park, 277 Bin Yang Road, Tiandeng County, Chongzuo, Guangxi Autonomous Region. Postal Code: 316061. Phone Number：11859821. E-mail：edqfr@sqczebto.parks.cn

1417。姓名: 赏骥易

住址（博物院）：广西壮族自治区桂林市雁山区友南路 682 号桂林博物馆（邮政编码：867826）。联系电话：59519868。电子邮箱：agkvw@ucrebzjf.museums.cn

Zhù zhǐ: Shǎng Jì Yì Guǎngxī Zhuàngzú Zìzhìqū Guìlín Shì Yàn Shānqū Yǒu Nán Lù 682 Hào Gulín Bó Wù Guǎn（Yóuzhèng Biānmǎ：867826）. Liánxì Diànhuà：59519868. Diànzǐ Yóuxiāng： agkvw@ucrebzjf.museums.cn

Ji Yi Shang, Guilin Museum, 682 You Nan Road, Yanshan District, Guilin, Guangxi Autonomous Region. Postal Code: 867826. Phone Number：59519868. E-mail：agkvw@ucrebzjf.museums.cn

1418。姓名: 纪铁红

住址（酒店）：广西壮族自治区贵港市平南县龙化路 607 号全黎酒店（邮政编码：345630）。联系电话：98520215。电子邮箱：zdvkq@vojemhsr.biz.cn

Zhù zhǐ: Jì Tiě Hóng Guǎngxī Zhuàngzú Zìzhìqū Guìgǎng Shì Píng Nán Xiàn Lóng Huā Lù 607 Hào Quán Lí Jiǔ Diàn（Yóuzhèng Biānmǎ：345630）. Liánxì Diànhuà：98520215. Diànzǐ Yóuxiāng： zdvkq@vojemhsr.biz.cn

Tie Hong Ji, Quan Li Hotel, 607 Long Hua Road, Pingnan County, Guigang, Guangxi Autonomous Region. Postal Code: 345630. Phone Number：98520215. E-mail：zdvkq@vojemhsr.biz.cn

1419。姓名: 柯智盛

住址（酒店）：广西壮族自治区桂林市秀峰区德舟路 703 号帆铁酒店（邮政编码：145052）。联系电话：19481730。电子邮箱：knqom@sepdyfzt.biz.cn

Zhù zhǐ: Kē Zhì Chéng Guǎngxī Zhuàngzú Zìzhìqū Guìlín Shì Xiùfēng Qū Dé Zhōu Lù 703 Hào Fān Tiě Jiǔ Diàn（Yóuzhèng Biānmǎ：145052）. Liánxì Diànhuà：19481730. Diànzǐ Yóuxiāng：knqom@sepdyfzt.biz.cn

Zhi Cheng Ke, Fan Tie Hotel, 703 De Zhou Road, Xiufeng District, Guilin, Guangxi Autonomous Region. Postal Code: 145052. Phone Number：19481730. E-mail：knqom@sepdyfzt.biz.cn

1420。姓名: 樊骥迅

住址（家庭）：广西壮族自治区崇左市龙州县冕领路 637 号土亚公寓 31 层 197 室（邮政编码：395534）。联系电话：73273075。电子邮箱：tjkwn@hdbugjmw.cn

Zhù zhǐ: Fán Jì Xùn Guǎngxī Zhuàngzú Zìzhìqū Chóng Zuǒ Shì Lóng Zhōu Xiàn Miǎn Lǐng Lù 637 Hào Tǔ Yà Gōng Yù 31 Céng 197 Shì (Yóuzhèng Biānmǎ：395534). Liánxì Diànhuà：73273075. Diànzǐ Yóuxiāng：tjkwn@hdbugjmw.cn

Ji Xun Fan, Room# 197, Floor# 31, Tu Ya Apartment, 637 Mian Ling Road, Longzhou County, Chongzuo, Guangxi Autonomous Region. Postal Code: 395534. Phone Number：73273075. E-mail：tjkwn@hdbugjmw.cn

1421。姓名: 齐土辉

住址（湖泊）：广西壮族自治区梧州市藤县化化路 393 号稼晖湖（邮政编码：214099）。联系电话：98425230。电子邮箱：miowl@zblthnvr.lakes.cn

Zhù zhǐ: Qí Tǔ Huī Guǎngxī Zhuàngzú Zìzhìqū Wúzhōu Shì Téng Xiàn Huà Huà Lù 393 Hào Jià Huī Hú (Yóuzhèng Biānmǎ: 214099). Liánxì Diànhuà: 98425230. Diànzǐ Yóuxiāng: miowl@zblthnvr.lakes.cn

Tu Hui Qi, Jia Hui Lake, 393 Hua Hua Road, Fuji County, Wuzhou, Guangxi Autonomous Region. Postal Code: 214099. Phone Number: 98425230. E-mail: miowl@zblthnvr.lakes.cn

1422。姓名: 商可科

住址（湖泊）：广西壮族自治区桂林市恭城瑶族自治县土立路 638 号愈员湖（邮政编码：891577）。联系电话：21916452。电子邮箱：houye@hzauynlr.lakes.cn

Zhù zhǐ: Shāng Kě Kē Guǎngxī Zhuàngzú Zìzhìqū Guìlín Shì Gōng Chéng Yáozú Zìzhìxiàn Tǔ Lì Lù 638 Hào Yù Yuán Hú (Yóuzhèng Biānmǎ: 891577). Liánxì Diànhuà: 21916452. Diànzǐ Yóuxiāng: houye@hzauynlr.lakes.cn

Ke Ke Shang, Yu Yuan Lake, 638 Tu Li Road, Gongcheng Yao Autonomous County, Guilin, Guangxi Autonomous Region. Postal Code: 891577. Phone Number: 21916452. E-mail: houye@hzauynlr.lakes.cn

1423。姓名: 琴大渊

住址（家庭）：广西壮族自治区玉林市兴业县坡黎路 974 号员翼公寓 16 层 370 室（邮政编码：980468）。联系电话：17107331。电子邮箱：dqayb@jblaqeyu.cn

Zhù zhǐ: Qín Dài Yuān Guǎngxī Zhuàngzú Zìzhìqū Yùlín Shì Xìngyè Xiàn Pō Lí Lù 974 Hào Yún Yì Gōng Yù 16 Céng 370 Shì (Yóuzhèng Biānmǎ: 980468). Liánxì Diànhuà: 17107331. Diànzǐ Yóuxiāng: dqayb@jblaqeyu.cn

Dai Yuan Qin, Room# 370, Floor# 16, Yun Yi Apartment, 974 Po Li Road, Xingye County, Yulin, Guangxi Autonomous Region. Postal Code: 980468. Phone Number: 17107331. E-mail: dqayb@jblaqeyu.cn

1424。姓名: 简钢坚

住址（湖泊）：广西壮族自治区钦州市钦南区计领路 330 号自茂湖（邮政编码：286600）。联系电话：27048015。电子邮箱：qwcgf@hoqntlfm.lakes.cn

Zhù zhǐ: Jiǎn Gāng Jiān Guǎngxī Zhuàngzú Zìzhìqū Qīnzhōu Shì Qīn Nán Qū Jì Lǐng Lù 330 Hào Zì Mào Hú (Yóuzhèng Biānmǎ：286600). Liánxì Diànhuà：27048015. Diànzǐ Yóuxiāng：qwcgf@hoqntlfm.lakes.cn

Gang Jian Jian, Zi Mao Lake, 330 Ji Ling Road, Chennan District, Qinzhou, Guangxi Autonomous Region. Postal Code: 286600. Phone Number：27048015. E-mail：qwcgf@hoqntlfm.lakes.cn

1425。姓名: 酆奎己

住址（医院）：广西壮族自治区玉林市福绵区郁仓路 252 号仲跃医院（邮政编码：127209）。联系电话：27402985。电子邮箱：lteqc@aenwmubj.health.cn

Zhù zhǐ: Fēng Kuí Jǐ Guǎngxī Zhuàngzú Zìzhìqū Yùlín Shì Fú Mián Qū Yù Cāng Lù 252 Hào Zhòng Yuè Yī Yuàn (Yóuzhèng Biānmǎ：127209). Liánxì Diànhuà：27402985. Diànzǐ Yóuxiāng：lteqc@aenwmubj.health.cn

Kui Ji Feng, Zhong Yue Hospital, 252 Yu Cang Road, Fumian District, Yulin, Guangxi Autonomous Region. Postal Code: 127209. Phone Number：27402985. E-mail：lteqc@aenwmubj.health.cn

1426。姓名: 冷大翰

住址（湖泊）：广西壮族自治区防城港市港口区桥源路 818 号臻祥湖（邮政编码：647882）。联系电话：44118927。电子邮箱：gukam@wqmnsbkp.lakes.cn

Zhù zhǐ: Lěng Dài Hàn Guǎngxī Zhuàngzú Zìzhìqū Fángchénggǎng Shì Gǎngkǒu Qū Qiáo Yuán Lù 818 Hào Zhēn Xiáng Hú (Yóuzhèng Biānmǎ：647882). Liánxì Diànhuà：44118927. Diànzǐ Yóuxiāng：gukam@wqmnsbkp.lakes.cn

Dai Han Leng, Zhen Xiang Lake, 818 Qiao Yuan Road, Port Area, Fangchenggang, Guangxi Autonomous Region. Postal Code: 647882. Phone Number：44118927. E-mail：gukam@wqmnsbkp.lakes.cn

1427。姓名: 巢福沛

住址（湖泊）：广西壮族自治区玉林市北流市冕土路 363 号伦珏湖（邮政编码：635562）。联系电话：55223533。电子邮箱：yoxcp@gembysqk.lakes.cn

Zhù zhǐ: Cháo Fú Pèi Guǎngxī Zhuàngzú Zìzhìqū Yùlín Shì Běi Liú Shì Miǎn Tǔ Lù 363 Hào Lún Jué Hú（Yóuzhèng Biānmǎ：635562). Liánxì Diànhuà：55223533. Diànzǐ Yóuxiāng：yoxcp@gembysqk.lakes.cn

Fu Pei Chao, Lun Jue Lake, 363 Mian Tu Road, Beiliu, Yulin, Guangxi Autonomous Region. Postal Code: 635562. Phone Number：55223533. E-mail：yoxcp@gembysqk.lakes.cn

1428。姓名: 戴陆豪

住址（家庭）：广西壮族自治区南宁市横州市毅浩路 425 号亚跃公寓 1 层 746 室（邮政编码：302572）。联系电话：93797108。电子邮箱：nmexi@bmwjrflz.cn

Zhù zhǐ: Dài Liù Háo Guǎngxī Zhuàngzú Zìzhìqū Nánníng Shì Héng Zhōu Shì Yì Hào Lù 425 Hào Yà Yuè Gōng Yù 1 Céng 746 Shì (Yóuzhèng Biānmǎ：302572). Liánxì Diànhuà：93797108. Diànzǐ Yóuxiāng：nmexi@bmwjrflz.cn

Liu Hao Dai, Room# 746, Floor# 1, Ya Yue Apartment, 425 Yi Hao Road, Hengzhou, NanNing, Guangxi Autonomous Region. Postal Code: 302572. Phone Number：93797108. E-mail：nmexi@bmwjrflz.cn

1429。姓名: 翟发亭

住址（公共汽车站）：广西壮族自治区来宾市金秀瑶族自治县跃兆路 442 号翰不站（邮政编码：256328）。联系电话：74938960。电子邮箱：dawcp@bvaotdku.transport.cn

Zhù zhǐ: Zhái Fā Tíng Guǎngxī Zhuàngzú Zìzhìqū Láibīn Shì Jīn Xiù Yáozú Zìzhìxiàn Yuè Zhào Lù 442 Hào Hàn Bù Zhàn (Yóuzhèng Biānmǎ: 256328). Liánxì Diànhuà: 74938960. Diànzǐ Yóuxiāng: dawcp@bvaotdku.transport.cn

Fa Ting Zhai, Han Bu Bus Station, 442 Yue Zhao Road, Jinxiu Yao Autonomous County, Laibin, Guangxi Autonomous Region. Postal Code: 256328. Phone Number: 74938960. E-mail: dawcp@bvaotdku.transport.cn

1430。姓名: 车立豪

住址（公司）：广西壮族自治区百色市田阳区涛楚路 329 号鸣宝有限公司（邮政编码：369915）。联系电话：19034963。电子邮箱：jzfcb@djmsiolk.biz.cn

Zhù zhǐ: Chē Lì Háo Guǎngxī Zhuàngzú Zìzhìqū Bǎisè Shì Tiányáng Qū Tāo Chǔ Lù 329 Hào Míng Bǎo Yǒuxiàn Gōngsī (Yóuzhèng Biānmǎ: 369915). Liánxì Diànhuà: 19034963. Diànzǐ Yóuxiāng: jzfcb@djmsiolk.biz.cn

Li Hao Che, Ming Bao Corporation, 329 Tao Chu Road, Tianyang District, Baise, Guangxi Autonomous Region. Postal Code: 369915. Phone Number: 19034963. E-mail: jzfcb@djmsiolk.biz.cn

1431。姓名: 冷辙国

住址（酒店）：广西壮族自治区河池市金城江区坡骥路 362 号愈征酒店（邮政编码：364452）。联系电话：18017292。电子邮箱：bzdqf@xmrzfpje.biz.cn

Zhù zhǐ: Lěng Zhé Guó Guǎngxī Zhuàngzú Zìzhìqū Héchí Shì Jīnchéng Jiāng Qū Pō Jì Lù 362 Hào Yù Zhēng Jiǔ Diàn (Yóuzhèng Biānmǎ: 364452). Liánxì Diànhuà: 18017292. Diànzǐ Yóuxiāng: bzdqf@xmrzfpje.biz.cn

Zhe Guo Leng, Yu Zheng Hotel, 362 Po Ji Road, Jinchengjiang District, Hechi, Guangxi Autonomous Region. Postal Code: 364452. Phone Number: 18017292. E-mail: bzdqf@xmrzfpje.biz.cn

1432。姓名: 罗智化

住址（医院）：广西壮族自治区贺州市钟山县红学路 936 号世民医院（邮政编码：302719）。联系电话：58440720。电子邮箱：faivo@aygvsemf.health.cn

Zhù zhǐ: Luó Zhì Huà Guǎngxī Zhuàngzú Zìzhìqū Hèzhōu Shì Zhōng Shān Xiàn Hóng Xué Lù 936 Hào Shì Mín Yī Yuàn (Yóuzhèng Biānmǎ：302719). Liánxì Diànhuà：58440720. Diànzǐ Yóuxiāng：faivo@aygvsemf.health.cn

Zhi Hua Luo, Shi Min Hospital, 936 Hong Xue Road, Zhongshan County, Hezhou, Guangxi Autonomous Region. Postal Code: 302719. Phone Number：58440720. E-mail：faivo@aygvsemf.health.cn

1433。姓名: 臧近黎

住址（家庭）：广西壮族自治区柳州市融安县发咚路 209 号焯宽公寓 11 层 360 室（邮政编码：534940）。联系电话：45707673。电子邮箱：iscnj@wugfrcad.cn

Zhù zhǐ: Zāng Jìn Lí Guǎngxī Zhuàngzú Zìzhìqū Liǔzhōu Shì Róng Ānxiàn Fā Dōng Lù 209 Hào Zhuō Kuān Gōng Yù 11 Céng 360 Shì (Yóuzhèng Biānmǎ：534940). Liánxì Diànhuà：45707673. Diànzǐ Yóuxiāng：iscnj@wugfrcad.cn

Jin Li Zang, Room# 360, Floor# 11, Zhuo Kuan Apartment, 209 Fa Dong Road, Rongan County, Liuzhou, Guangxi Autonomous Region. Postal Code: 534940. Phone Number：45707673. E-mail：iscnj@wugfrcad.cn

1434。姓名: 侯寰风

住址（酒店）：广西壮族自治区玉林市福绵区谢铁路 788 号尚亚酒店（邮政编码：953452）。联系电话：20328744。电子邮箱：yhlxw@vwbnjdks.biz.cn

Zhù zhǐ: Hóu Huán Fēng Guǎngxī Zhuàngzú Zìzhìqū Yùlín Shì Fú Mián Qū Xiè Tiě Lù 788 Hào Shàng Yà Jiǔ Diàn (Yóuzhèng Biānmǎ：953452). Liánxì Diànhuà：20328744. Diànzǐ Yóuxiāng：yhlxw@vwbnjdks.biz.cn

Huan Feng Hou, Shang Ya Hotel, 788 Xie Tie Road, Fumian District, Yulin, Guangxi Autonomous Region. Postal Code: 953452. Phone Number：20328744. E-mail：yhlxw@vwbnjdks.biz.cn

1435。姓名: 益大金

住址（寺庙）：广西壮族自治区钦州市钦南区立近路 387 号进葛寺（邮政编码：453435）。联系电话：43176796。电子邮箱：wklhf@pvsltkxe.god.cn

Zhù zhǐ: Yì Dà Jīn Guǎngxī Zhuàngzú Zìzhìqū Qīnzhōu Shì Qīn Nán Qū Lì Jìn Lù 387 Hào Jìn Gé Sì (Yóuzhèng Biānmǎ：453435). Liánxì Diànhuà：43176796. Diànzǐ Yóuxiāng：wklhf@pvsltkxe.god.cn

Da Jin Yi, Jin Ge Temple, 387 Li Jin Road, Chennan District, Qinzhou, Guangxi Autonomous Region. Postal Code: 453435. Phone Number：43176796. E-mail：wklhf@pvsltkxe.god.cn

1436。姓名: 危近九

住址（公共汽车站）：广西壮族自治区百色市田阳区冕珂路 765 号计钢站（邮政编码：550423）。联系电话：99516916。电子邮箱：uklip@yabupdos.transport.cn

Zhù zhǐ: Wēi Jìn Jiǔ Guǎngxī Zhuàngzú Zìzhìqū Bǎisè Shì Tiányáng Qū Miǎn Kē Lù 765 Hào Jì Gāng Zhàn (Yóuzhèng Biānmǎ：550423). Liánxì Diànhuà：99516916. Diànzǐ Yóuxiāng：uklip@yabupdos.transport.cn

Jin Jiu Wei, Ji Gang Bus Station, 765 Mian Ke Road, Tianyang District, Baise, Guangxi Autonomous Region. Postal Code: 550423. Phone Number：99516916. E-mail：uklip@yabupdos.transport.cn

1437。姓名: 谭奎澜

住址（博物院）：广西壮族自治区河池市都安瑶族自治县近汉路 969 号河池博物馆（邮政编码：175480）。联系电话：49094927。电子邮箱：cprwd@shulxzvb.museums.cn

Zhù zhǐ: Tán Kuí Lán Guǎngxī Zhuàngzú Zìzhìqū Héchí Shì Dū Ān Yáozú Zìzhìxiàn Jìn Hàn Lù 969 Hào Hécí Bó Wù Guǎn （Yóuzhèng Biānmǎ：175480). Liánxì Diànhuà：49094927. Diànzǐ Yóuxiāng：cprwd@shulxzvb.museums.cn

Kui Lan Tan, Hechi Museum, 969 Jin Han Road, Duan Yao Autonomous County, Hechi, Guangxi Autonomous Region. Postal Code: 175480. Phone Number：49094927. E-mail：cprwd@shulxzvb.museums.cn

1438。姓名: 万焯泽

住址（酒店）：广西壮族自治区贺州市平桂区威铭路 493 号焯德酒店（邮政编码：692430）。联系电话：91866495。电子邮箱：dfwpc@khjmolur.biz.cn

Zhù zhǐ: Wàn Chāo Zé Guǎngxī Zhuàngzú Zìzhìqū Hèzhōu Shì Píng Guì Qū Wēi Míng Lù 493 Hào Chāo Dé Jiǔ Diàn （Yóuzhèng Biānmǎ：692430). Liánxì Diànhuà：91866495. Diànzǐ Yóuxiāng：dfwpc@khjmolur.biz.cn

Chao Ze Wan, Chao De Hotel, 493 Wei Ming Road, Pinggui District, Hezhou, Guangxi Autonomous Region. Postal Code: 692430. Phone Number：91866495. E-mail：dfwpc@khjmolur.biz.cn

1439。姓名: 别金惟

住址（博物院）：广西壮族自治区南宁市青秀区俊领路 503 号南宁博物馆（邮政编码：682624）。联系电话：59652343。电子邮箱：ntjfb@sdriayvj.museums.cn

Zhù zhǐ: Bié Jīn Wéi Guǎngxī Zhuàngzú Zìzhìqū Nánníng Shì Qīng Xiù Qū Jùn Lǐng Lù 503 Hào Nánníng Bó Wù Guǎn （Yóuzhèng Biānmǎ：682624). Liánxì Diànhuà：59652343. Diànzǐ Yóuxiāng：ntjfb@sdriayvj.museums.cn

Jin Wei Bie, NanNing Museum, 503 Jun Ling Road, Qingxiu District, NanNing, Guangxi Autonomous Region. Postal Code: 682624. Phone Number：59652343. E-mail：ntjfb@sdriayvj.museums.cn

1440。姓名: 单辉科

住址（火车站）：广西壮族自治区百色市隆林各族自治县涛冠路 535 号百色站（邮政编码：408789）。联系电话：14975899。电子邮箱：wfyel@ovhimkpy.chr.cn

Zhù zhǐ: Shàn Huī Kē Guǎngxī Zhuàngzú Zìzhìqū Bǎisè Shì Lóng Lín Gè Zú Zìzhìxiàn Tāo Guān Lù 535 Hào Bǎisè Zhàn (Yóuzhèng Biānmǎ：408789). Liánxì Diànhuà：14975899. Diànzǐ Yóuxiāng：wfyel@ovhimkpy.chr.cn

Hui Ke Shan, Baise Railway Station, 535 Tao Guan Road, Longlin Autonomous County Of Various Nationalities, Baise, Guangxi Autonomous Region. Postal Code: 408789. Phone Number：14975899. E-mail：wfyel@ovhimkpy.chr.cn

CHAPTER 4: NAME, SURNAME & ADDRESSES (91-120)

1441。姓名: 闵辙全

住址（家庭）：广西壮族自治区钦州市钦北区原昌路 686 号食楚公寓 44 层 899 室（邮政编码：465753）。联系电话：61035622。电子邮箱：jrxkv@cygktbfa.cn

Zhù zhǐ: Mǐn Zhé Quán Guǎngxī Zhuàngzú Zìzhìqū Qīnzhōu Shì Qīn Běi Qū Yuán Chāng Lù 686 Hào Sì Chǔ Gōng Yù 44 Céng 899 Shì (Yóuzhèng Biānmǎ：465753). Liánxì Diànhuà：61035622. Diànzǐ Yóuxiāng：jrxkv@cygktbfa.cn

Zhe Quan Min, Room# 899, Floor# 44, Si Chu Apartment, 686 Yuan Chang Road, Qinbei District, Qinzhou, Guangxi Autonomous Region. Postal Code: 465753. Phone Number：61035622. E-mail：jrxkv@cygktbfa.cn

1442。姓名: 曹尚隆

住址（博物院）：广西壮族自治区贵港市覃塘区咚员路 488 号贵港博物馆（邮政编码：666811）。联系电话：62731110。电子邮箱：xzopd@grjetial.museums.cn

Zhù zhǐ: Cáo Shàng Lóng Guǎngxī Zhuàngzú Zìzhìqū Guìgǎng Shì Tán Táng Qū Dōng Yún Lù 488 Hào Gugǎng Bó Wù Guǎn (Yóuzhèng Biānmǎ：666811). Liánxì Diànhuà：62731110. Diànzǐ Yóuxiāng：xzopd@grjetial.museums.cn

Shang Long Cao, Guigang Museum, 488 Dong Yun Road, Qintang District, Guigang, Guangxi Autonomous Region. Postal Code: 666811. Phone Number：62731110. E-mail：xzopd@grjetial.museums.cn

1443。姓名: 虞陆熔

住址（酒店）：广西壮族自治区贵港市桂平市迅桥路 864 号成国酒店（邮政编码：280542）。联系电话：57548271。电子邮箱：aumsw@gmtparez.biz.cn

Zhù zhǐ: Yú Liù Róng Guǎngxī Zhuàngzú Zìzhìqū Guìgǎng Shì Guìpíngshì Xùn Qiáo Lù 864 Hào Chéng Guó Jiǔ Diàn (Yóuzhèng Biānmǎ: 280542). Liánxì Diànhuà: 57548271. Diànzǐ Yóuxiāng: aumsw@gmtparez.biz.cn

Liu Rong Yu, Cheng Guo Hotel, 864 Xun Qiao Road, Guiping, Guigang, Guangxi Autonomous Region. Postal Code: 280542. Phone Number: 57548271. E-mail: aumsw@gmtparez.biz.cn

1444。姓名: 左郁振

住址（博物院）：广西壮族自治区桂林市全州县葆锡路 925 号桂林博物馆（邮政编码：148272）。联系电话：72506539。电子邮箱：gbiot@pfxwribv.museums.cn

Zhù zhǐ: Zuǒ Yù Zhèn Guǎngxī Zhuàngzú Zìzhìqū Guìlín Shì Quán Zhōu Xiàn Bǎo Xī Lù 925 Hào Gulín Bó Wù Guǎn (Yóuzhèng Biānmǎ: 148272). Liánxì Diànhuà: 72506539. Diànzǐ Yóuxiāng: gbiot@pfxwribv.museums.cn

Yu Zhen Zuo, Guilin Museum, 925 Bao Xi Road, Quanzhou County, Guilin, Guangxi Autonomous Region. Postal Code: 148272. Phone Number: 72506539. E-mail: gbiot@pfxwribv.museums.cn

1445。姓名: 伍国水

住址（医院）：广西壮族自治区北海市海城区食钦路 954 号懂渊医院（邮政编码：897062）。联系电话：80730639。电子邮箱：ndqkh@fpondzkw.health.cn

Zhù zhǐ: Wǔ Guó Shuǐ Guǎngxī Zhuàngzú Zìzhìqū Běihǎi Shì Hǎi Chéngqū Yì Qīn Lù 954 Hào Dǒng Yuān Yī Yuàn (Yóuzhèng Biānmǎ: 897062). Liánxì Diànhuà: 80730639. Diànzǐ Yóuxiāng: ndqkh@fpondzkw.health.cn

Guo Shui Wu, Dong Yuan Hospital, 954 Yi Qin Road, Haicheng District, Beihai, Guangxi Autonomous Region. Postal Code: 897062. Phone Number: 80730639. E-mail: ndqkh@fpondzkw.health.cn

1446。姓名: 曹德辙

住址（公共汽车站）：广西壮族自治区钦州市浦北县智威路 759 号阳中站
（邮政编码：881998）。联系电话：19920819。电子邮箱：
gbxpo@tkapixro.transport.cn

Zhù zhǐ: Cáo Dé Zhé Guǎngxī Zhuàngzú Zìzhìqū Qīnzhōu Shì Pǔ Běi Xiàn Zhì Wēi Lù
759 Hào Yáng Zhōng Zhàn（Yóuzhèng Biānmǎ：881998). Liánxì Diànhuà：
19920819. Diànzǐ Yóuxiāng：gbxpo@tkapixro.transport.cn

De Zhe Cao, Yang Zhong Bus Station, 759 Zhi Wei Road, Pubei County, Qinzhou,
Guangxi Autonomous Region. Postal Code: 881998. Phone Number：19920819.
E-mail：gbxpo@tkapixro.transport.cn

1447。姓名: 尚辙成

住址（湖泊）：广西壮族自治区柳州市柳江区盛懂路 239 号队智湖（邮政编
码：495965）。联系电话：35750354。电子邮箱：hcwzu@cgdxihwo.lakes.cn

Zhù zhǐ: Shàng Zhé Chéng Guǎngxī Zhuàngzú Zìzhìqū Liǔzhōu Shì Liǔjiāng Qū Shèng
Dǒng Lù 239 Hào Duì Zhì Hú（Yóuzhèng Biānmǎ：495965). Liánxì Diànhuà：
35750354. Diànzǐ Yóuxiāng：hcwzu@cgdxihwo.lakes.cn

Zhe Cheng Shang, Dui Zhi Lake, 239 Sheng Dong Road, Liujiang District, Liuzhou,
Guangxi Autonomous Region. Postal Code: 495965. Phone Number：35750354.
E-mail：hcwzu@cgdxihwo.lakes.cn

1448。姓名: 齐仓珂

住址（寺庙）：广西壮族自治区百色市右江区熔己路 156 号寰祥寺（邮政编
码：624396）。联系电话：42720718。电子邮箱：hjqkm@icejgxuv.god.cn

Zhù zhǐ: Qí Cāng Kē Guǎngxī Zhuàngzú Zìzhìqū Bǎisè Shì Yòu Jiāng Qū Róng Jǐ Lù
156 Hào Huán Xiáng Sì（Yóuzhèng Biānmǎ：624396). Liánxì Diànhuà：42720718.
Diànzǐ Yóuxiāng：hjqkm@icejgxuv.god.cn

Cang Ke Qi, Huan Xiang Temple, 156 Rong Ji Road, Youjiang District, Baise, Guangxi Autonomous Region. Postal Code: 624396. Phone Number：42720718. E-mail：hjqkm@icejgxuv.god.cn

1449。姓名: 应阳游

住址（家庭）：广西壮族自治区来宾市合山市成守路 421 号坤可公寓 49 层 323 室（邮政编码：294144）。联系电话：28489946。电子邮箱：hdwqg@pergqhvk.cn

Zhù zhǐ: Yīng Yáng Yóu Guǎngxī Zhuàngzú Zìzhìqū Láibīn Shì Hé Shān Shì Chéng Shǒu Lù 421 Hào Kūn Kě Gōng Yù 49 Céng 323 Shì (Yóuzhèng Biānmǎ：294144). Liánxì Diànhuà：28489946. Diànzǐ Yóuxiāng：hdwqg@pergqhvk.cn

Yang You Ying, Room# 323, Floor# 49, Kun Ke Apartment, 421 Cheng Shou Road, Heshan City, Laibin, Guangxi Autonomous Region. Postal Code: 294144. Phone Number：28489946. E-mail：hdwqg@pergqhvk.cn

1450。姓名: 夔亭甫

住址（家庭）：广西壮族自治区崇左市江州区兵智路 556 号龙跃公寓 43 层 913 室（邮政编码：500546）。联系电话：69141680。电子邮箱：lwkce@fjrhecdz.cn

Zhù zhǐ: Kuí Tíng Fǔ Guǎngxī Zhuàngzú Zìzhìqū Chóng Zuǒ Shì Jiāng Zhōu Qū Bīng Zhì Lù 556 Hào Lóng Yuè Gōng Yù 43 Céng 913 Shì (Yóuzhèng Biānmǎ：500546). Liánxì Diànhuà：69141680. Diànzǐ Yóuxiāng：lwkce@fjrhecdz.cn

Ting Fu Kui, Room# 913, Floor# 43, Long Yue Apartment, 556 Bing Zhi Road, Jiangzhou District, Chongzuo, Guangxi Autonomous Region. Postal Code: 500546. Phone Number：69141680. E-mail：lwkce@fjrhecdz.cn

1451。姓名: 叶辉昌

住址（大学）：广西壮族自治区北海市海城区锡游大学俊食路 938 号（邮政编码：390148）。联系电话：97858980。电子邮箱：phmnl@vmhpfyzt.edu.cn

Zhù zhǐ: Yè Huī Chāng Guǎngxī Zhuàngzú Zìzhìqū Běihǎi Shì Hǎi Chéngqū Xī Yóu DàxuéJùn Sì Lù 938 Hào (Yóuzhèng Biānmǎ: 390148). Liánxì Diànhuà: 97858980. Diànzǐ Yóuxiāng: phmnl@vmhpfyzt.edu.cn

Hui Chang Ye, Xi You University, 938 Jun Si Road, Haicheng District, Beihai, Guangxi Autonomous Region. Postal Code: 390148. Phone Number: 97858980. E-mail: phmnl@vmhpfyzt.edu.cn

1452。姓名:呼延学石

住址（公共汽车站）：广西壮族自治区北海市银海区恩庆路 207 号翰毅站（邮政编码：295889）。联系电话：36119531。电子邮箱：rwcqg@xhwzmigy.transport.cn

Zhù zhǐ: Hūyán Xué Shí Guǎngxī Zhuàngzú Zìzhìqū Běihǎi Shì Yín Hǎi Qū Ēn Qìng Lù 207 Hào Hàn Yì Zhàn (Yóuzhèng Biānmǎ: 295889). Liánxì Diànhuà: 36119531. Diànzǐ Yóuxiāng: rwcqg@xhwzmigy.transport.cn

Xue Shi Huyan, Han Yi Bus Station, 207 En Qing Road, Yinhai District, Beihai, Guangxi Autonomous Region. Postal Code: 295889. Phone Number: 36119531. E-mail: rwcqg@xhwzmigy.transport.cn

1453。姓名:骆大郁

住址（公司）：广西壮族自治区南宁市邕宁区兆其路 894 号沛自有限公司（邮政编码：746248）。联系电话：86589207。电子邮箱：qrait@avxfwecl.biz.cn

Zhù zhǐ: Luò Dà Yù Guǎngxī Zhuàngzú Zìzhìqū Nánníng Shì Yōng Níng Qū Zhào Qí Lù 894 Hào Pèi Zì Yǒuxiàn Gōngsī (Yóuzhèng Biānmǎ: 746248). Liánxì Diànhuà: 86589207. Diànzǐ Yóuxiāng: qrait@avxfwecl.biz.cn

Da Yu Luo, Pei Zi Corporation, 894 Zhao Qi Road, Yongning District, NanNing, Guangxi Autonomous Region. Postal Code: 746248. Phone Number: 86589207. E-mail: qrait@avxfwecl.biz.cn

1454。姓名: 左丘亚强

住址（广场）：广西壮族自治区防城港市上思县土亮路 919 号铁跃广场（邮政编码：331641）。联系电话：52917023。电子邮箱：paefl@ujrqnysw.squares.cn

Zhù zhǐ: Zuǒqiū Yà Qiáng Guǎngxī Zhuàngzú Zìzhìqū Fángchénggǎng Shì Shàng Sī Xiàn Tǔ Liàng Lù 919 Hào Fū Yuè Guǎng Chǎng (Yóuzhèng Biānmǎ：331641). Liánxì Diànhuà：52917023. Diànzǐ Yóuxiāng：paefl@ujrqnysw.squares.cn

Ya Qiang Zuoqiu, Fu Yue Square, 919 Tu Liang Road, Shangsi County, Fangchenggang, Guangxi Autonomous Region. Postal Code: 331641. Phone Number：52917023. E-mail：paefl@ujrqnysw.squares.cn

1455。姓名: 诸仓钢

住址（酒店）：广西壮族自治区河池市环江毛南族自治县谢化路 780 号中民酒店（邮政编码：847546）。联系电话：95081667。电子邮箱：wyilo@qrvjnoig.biz.cn

Zhù zhǐ: Zhū Cāng Gāng Guǎngxī Zhuàngzú Zìzhìqū Héchí Shì Huán Jiāng Máonán Zú Zìzhìxiàn Xiè Huà Lù 780 Hào Zhòng Mín Jiǔ Diàn (Yóuzhèng Biānmǎ：847546). Liánxì Diànhuà：95081667. Diànzǐ Yóuxiāng：wyilo@qrvjnoig.biz.cn

Cang Gang Zhu, Zhong Min Hotel, 780 Xie Hua Road, Huanjiang Maonan Autonomous County, Hechi, Guangxi Autonomous Region. Postal Code: 847546. Phone Number：95081667. E-mail：wyilo@qrvjnoig.biz.cn

1456。姓名: 范员九

住址（医院）：广西壮族自治区来宾市金秀瑶族自治县黎黎路 984 号际际医院（邮政编码：687262）。联系电话：57967785。电子邮箱：ovmfl@hrwksmoj.health.cn

Zhù zhǐ: Fàn Yún Jiǔ Guǎngxī Zhuàngzú Zìzhìqū Láibīn Shì Jīn Xiù Yáozú Zìzhìxiàn Lí Lí Lù 984 Hào Jì Jì Yī Yuàn (Yóuzhèng Biānmǎ: 687262). Liánxì Diànhuà: 57967785. Diànzǐ Yóuxiāng: ovmfl@hrwksmoj.health.cn

Yun Jiu Fan, Ji Ji Hospital, 984 Li Li Road, Jinxiu Yao Autonomous County, Laibin, Guangxi Autonomous Region. Postal Code: 687262. Phone Number: 57967785. E-mail: ovmfl@hrwksmoj.health.cn

1457。姓名: 刁斌德

住址（大学）：广西壮族自治区南宁市江南区浩愈大学科坤路 789 号（邮政编码：340872）。联系电话：48566810。电子邮箱：mhavx@laumytvd.edu.cn

Zhù zhǐ: Diāo Bīn Dé Guǎngxī Zhuàngzú Zìzhìqū Nánníng Shì Jiāngnán Qū Hào Yù DàxuéKē Kūn Lù 789 Hào (Yóuzhèng Biānmǎ: 340872). Liánxì Diànhuà: 48566810. Diànzǐ Yóuxiāng: mhavx@laumytvd.edu.cn

Bin De Diao, Hao Yu University, 789 Ke Kun Road, Gangnam District, NanNing, Guangxi Autonomous Region. Postal Code: 340872. Phone Number: 48566810. E-mail: mhavx@laumytvd.edu.cn

1458。姓名: 索秀跃

住址（公共汽车站）：广西壮族自治区贺州市富川瑶族自治县辙石路 950 号郁陆站（邮政编码：766499）。联系电话：14066251。电子邮箱：axejp@satkzgud.transport.cn

Zhù zhǐ: Suǒ Xiù Yuè Guǎngxī Zhuàngzú Zìzhìqū Hèzhōu Shì Fùchuān Yáozú Zìzhìxiàn Zhé Dàn Lù 950 Hào Yù Liù Zhàn (Yóuzhèng Biānmǎ: 766499). Liánxì Diànhuà: 14066251. Diànzǐ Yóuxiāng: axejp@satkzgud.transport.cn

Xiu Yue Suo, Yu Liu Bus Station, 950 Zhe Dan Road, Fuchuan Yao Autonomous County, Hezhou, Guangxi Autonomous Region. Postal Code: 766499. Phone Number: 14066251. E-mail: axejp@satkzgud.transport.cn

1459。姓名：逢翼仓

住址（医院）：广西壮族自治区梧州市长洲区仓宝路 431 号盛锤医院（邮政编码：594183）。联系电话：88233099。电子邮箱：jcwqa@tkedqxpa.health.cn

Zhù zhǐ: Páng Yì Cāng Guǎngxī Zhuàngzú Zìzhìqū Wúzhōu Shì Zhǎng Zhōu Qū Cāng Bǎo Lù 431 Hào Shèng Chuí Yī Yuàn（Yóuzhèng Biānmǎ：594183）. Liánxì Diànhuà：88233099. Diànzǐ Yóuxiāng：jcwqa@tkedqxpa.health.cn

Yi Cang Pang, Sheng Chui Hospital, 431 Cang Bao Road, Cheung Chau District, Wuzhou, Guangxi Autonomous Region. Postal Code: 594183. Phone Number：88233099. E-mail：jcwqa@tkedqxpa.health.cn

1460。姓名：支毅员

住址（机场）：广西壮族自治区百色市西林县龙翰路 211 号百色风亮国际机场（邮政编码：966626）。联系电话：31644720。电子邮箱：pfrzx@tslhgvqu.airports.cn

Zhù zhǐ: Zhī Yì Yuán Guǎngxī Zhuàngzú Zìzhìqū Bǎisè Shì Xīlín Xiàn Lóng Hàn Lù 211 Hào Bǎisè Fēng Liàng Guó Jì Jī Chǎng（Yóuzhèng Biānmǎ：966626）. Liánxì Diànhuà：31644720. Diànzǐ Yóuxiāng：pfrzx@tslhgvqu.airports.cn

Yi Yuan Zhi, Baise Feng Liang International Airport, 211 Long Han Road, Xilin County, Baise, Guangxi Autonomous Region. Postal Code: 966626. Phone Number：31644720. E-mail：pfrzx@tslhgvqu.airports.cn

1461。姓名：岳员铁

住址（酒店）：广西壮族自治区百色市田林县不盛路 176 号岐迅酒店（邮政编码：582482）。联系电话：19192641。电子邮箱：hgfte@bwafcqzo.biz.cn

Zhù zhǐ: Yuè Yuán Tiě Guǎngxī Zhuàngzú Zìzhìqū Bǎisè Shì Tiánlín Xiàn Bù Chéng Lù 176 Hào Qí Xùn Jiǔ Diàn（Yóuzhèng Biānmǎ：582482）. Liánxì Diànhuà：19192641. Diànzǐ Yóuxiāng：hgfte@bwafcqzo.biz.cn

Yuan Tie Yue, Qi Xun Hotel, 176 Bu Cheng Road, Tianlin County, Baise, Guangxi Autonomous Region. Postal Code: 582482. Phone Number：19192641. E-mail：hgfte@bwafcqzo.biz.cn

1462。姓名: 隆渊来

住址（寺庙）：广西壮族自治区来宾市象州县坚腾路 265 号铁亮寺（邮政编码：779138）。联系电话：20729805。电子邮箱：lmbis@bltgshmu.god.cn

Zhù zhǐ: Lóng Yuān Lái Guǎngxī Zhuàngzú Zìzhìqū Láibīn Shì Xiàng Zhōu Xiàn Jiān Téng Lù 265 Hào Tiě Liàng Sì（Yóuzhèng Biānmǎ：779138). Liánxì Diànhuà：20729805. Diànzǐ Yóuxiāng：lmbis@bltgshmu.god.cn

Yuan Lai Long, Tie Liang Temple, 265 Jian Teng Road, Xiangzhou County, Laibin, Guangxi Autonomous Region. Postal Code: 779138. Phone Number：20729805. E-mail：lmbis@bltgshmu.god.cn

1463。姓名: 单胜禹

住址（大学）：广西壮族自治区北海市铁山港区来自大学跃强路 155 号（邮政编码：681892）。联系电话：12842991。电子邮箱：nmxlg@sajlqpzr.edu.cn

Zhù zhǐ: Shàn Shēng Yǔ Guǎngxī Zhuàngzú Zìzhìqū Běihǎi Shì Tiě Shān Gǎng Qū Lái Zì DàxuéYuè Qiǎng Lù 155 Hào（Yóuzhèng Biānmǎ：681892). Liánxì Diànhuà：12842991. Diànzǐ Yóuxiāng：nmxlg@sajlqpzr.edu.cn

Sheng Yu Shan, Lai Zi University, 155 Yue Qiang Road, Iron Mountain Port District, Beihai, Guangxi Autonomous Region. Postal Code: 681892. Phone Number：12842991. E-mail：nmxlg@sajlqpzr.edu.cn

1464。姓名: 褚磊可

住址（机场）：广西壮族自治区百色市隆林各族自治县炯克路 291 号百色征食国际机场（邮政编码：757180）。联系电话：96300309。电子邮箱：ikuzn@gwezbaqt.airports.cn

Zhù zhǐ: Chǔ Lěi Kě Guǎngxī Zhuàngzú Zìzhìqū Bǎisè Shì Lóng Lín Gè Zú Zìzhìxiàn Jiǒng Kè Lù 291 Hào Bǎisè Zhēng Yì Guó Jì Jī Chǎng（Yóuzhèng Biānmǎ：757180）. Liánxì Diànhuà：96300309. Diànzǐ Yóuxiāng：ikuzn@gwezbaqt.airports.cn

Lei Ke Chu, Baise Zheng Yi International Airport, 291 Jiong Ke Road, Longlin Autonomous County Of Various Nationalities, Baise, Guangxi Autonomous Region. Postal Code: 757180. Phone Number：96300309. E-mail：ikuzn@gwezbaqt.airports.cn

1465。姓名: 咸迅翼

住址（公共汽车站）：广西壮族自治区百色市田东县磊谢路 475 号骥屹站（邮政编码：757084）。联系电话：38438738。电子邮箱：mafie@ajwfmbpi.transport.cn

Zhù zhǐ: Xián Xùn Yì Guǎngxī Zhuàngzú Zìzhìqū Bǎisè Shì Tián Dōng Xiàn Lěi Xiè Lù 475 Hào Jì Yì Zhàn（Yóuzhèng Biānmǎ：757084）. Liánxì Diànhuà：38438738. Diànzǐ Yóuxiāng：mafie@ajwfmbpi.transport.cn

Xun Yi Xian, Ji Yi Bus Station, 475 Lei Xie Road, Tiandong County, Baise, Guangxi Autonomous Region. Postal Code: 757084. Phone Number：38438738. E-mail：mafie@ajwfmbpi.transport.cn

1466。姓名: 葛其队

住址（公司）：广西壮族自治区北海市银海区葛楚路 434 号己豹有限公司（邮政编码：933279）。联系电话：80120299。电子邮箱：xpeys@mblhnjvw.biz.cn

Zhù zhǐ: Gě Qí Duì Guǎngxī Zhuàngzú Zìzhìqū Běihǎi Shì Yín Hǎi Qū Gé Chǔ Lù 434 Hào Jǐ Bào Yǒuxiàn Gōngsī（Yóuzhèng Biānmǎ：933279）. Liánxì Diànhuà：80120299. Diànzǐ Yóuxiāng：xpeys@mblhnjvw.biz.cn

Qi Dui Ge, Ji Bao Corporation, 434 Ge Chu Road, Yinhai District, Beihai, Guangxi Autonomous Region. Postal Code: 933279. Phone Number：80120299. E-mail：xpeys@mblhnjvw.biz.cn

1467。姓名: 齐乙俊

住址（家庭）：广西壮族自治区河池市环江毛南族自治县恩易路 304 号科成公寓 36 层 542 室（邮政编码：141416）。联系电话：43476182。电子邮箱：xmsfd@yskgnjle.cn

Zhù zhǐ: Qí Yǐ Jùn Guǎngxī Zhuàngzú Zìzhìqū Héchí Shì Huán Jiāng Máonán Zú Zìzhìxiàn Ēn Yì Lù 304 Hào Kē Chéng Gōng Yù 36 Céng 542 Shì (Yóuzhèng Biānmǎ: 141416). Liánxì Diànhuà：43476182. Diànzǐ Yóuxiāng：xmsfd@yskgnjle.cn

Yi Jun Qi, Room# 542, Floor# 36, Ke Cheng Apartment, 304 En Yi Road, Huanjiang Maonan Autonomous County, Hechi, Guangxi Autonomous Region. Postal Code: 141416. Phone Number：43476182. E-mail：xmsfd@yskgnjle.cn

1468。姓名: 乔兆轶

住址（公司）：广西壮族自治区防城港市东兴市顺食路 289 号楚锡有限公司（邮政编码：257809）。联系电话：19685311。电子邮箱：hdbfg@oxlwirsn.biz.cn

Zhù zhǐ: Qiáo Zhào Yì Guǎngxī Zhuàngzú Zìzhìqū Fángchénggǎng Shì Dōng Xīng Shì Shùn Sì Lù 289 Hào Chǔ Xī Yǒuxiàn Gōngsī (Yóuzhèng Biānmǎ: 257809). Liánxì Diànhuà：19685311. Diànzǐ Yóuxiāng：hdbfg@oxlwirsn.biz.cn

Zhao Yi Qiao, Chu Xi Corporation, 289 Shun Si Road, Dongxing City, Fangchenggang, Guangxi Autonomous Region. Postal Code: 257809. Phone Number：19685311. E-mail：hdbfg@oxlwirsn.biz.cn

1469。姓名: 靳强盛

住址（公司）：广西壮族自治区钦州市灵山县庆九路 424 号振陆有限公司（邮政编码：859763）。联系电话：80052333。电子邮箱：stgkc@rtfpcaew.biz.cn

Zhù zhǐ: Jìn Qiǎng Shèng Guǎngxī Zhuàngzú Zìzhìqū Qīnzhōu Shì Língshān Xiàn Qìng Jiǔ Lù 424 Hào Zhèn Lù Yǒuxiàn Gōngsī (Yóuzhèng Biānmǎ：859763). Liánxì Diànhuà：80052333. Diànzǐ Yóuxiāng：stgkc@rtfpcaew.biz.cn

Qiang Sheng Jin, Zhen Lu Corporation, 424 Qing Jiu Road, Lingshan County, Qinzhou, Guangxi Autonomous Region. Postal Code: 859763. Phone Number：80052333. E-mail：stgkc@rtfpcaew.biz.cn

1470。姓名: 管舟亭

住址（大学）：广西壮族自治区崇左市扶绥县乐轼大学斌学路 867 号（邮政编码：332132）。联系电话：30022383。电子邮箱：rgnqe@fuirbvcm.edu.cn

Zhù zhǐ: Guǎn Zhōu Tíng Guǎngxī Zhuàngzú Zìzhìqū Chóng Zuǒ Shì Fú Suí Xiàn Lè Shì DàxuéBīn Xué Lù 867 Hào (Yóuzhèng Biānmǎ：332132). Liánxì Diànhuà：30022383. Diànzǐ Yóuxiāng：rgnqe@fuirbvcm.edu.cn

Zhou Ting Guan, Le Shi University, 867 Bin Xue Road, Fusui County, Chongzuo, Guangxi Autonomous Region. Postal Code: 332132. Phone Number：30022383. E-mail：rgnqe@fuirbvcm.edu.cn

CHAPTER 5: NAME, SURNAME & ADDRESSES (121-150)

1471。姓名: 有乐科

住址（大学）：广西壮族自治区来宾市象州县冠进大学翰强路 928 号（邮政编码：386369）。联系电话：60273915。电子邮箱：iwgoc@cfvksjzw.edu.cn

Zhù zhǐ: Yǒu Lè Kē Guǎngxī Zhuàngzú Zìzhìqū Láibīn Shì Xiàng Zhōu Xiàn Guān Jìn DàxuéHàn Qiǎng Lù 928 Hào （Yóuzhèng Biānmǎ：386369). Liánxì Diànhuà：60273915. Diànzǐ Yóuxiāng：iwgoc@cfvksjzw.edu.cn

Le Ke You, Guan Jin University, 928 Han Qiang Road, Xiangzhou County, Laibin, Guangxi Autonomous Region. Postal Code: 386369. Phone Number：60273915. E-mail：iwgoc@cfvksjzw.edu.cn

1472。姓名: 乜盛屹

住址（寺庙）：广西壮族自治区北海市合浦县石沛路 392 号黎冠寺（邮政编码：969056）。联系电话：62446465。电子邮箱：zkgfr@fbpzdqvl.god.cn

Zhù zhǐ: Niè Chéng Yì Guǎngxī Zhuàngzú Zìzhìqū Běihǎi Shì Hépǔ Xiàn Dàn Bèi Lù 392 Hào Lí Guān Sì （Yóuzhèng Biānmǎ：969056). Liánxì Diànhuà：62446465. Diànzǐ Yóuxiāng：zkgfr@fbpzdqvl.god.cn

Cheng Yi Nie, Li Guan Temple, 392 Dan Bei Road, Hepu County, Beihai, Guangxi Autonomous Region. Postal Code: 969056. Phone Number：62446465. E-mail：zkgfr@fbpzdqvl.god.cn

1473。姓名: 晋宽守

住址（火车站）：广西壮族自治区南宁市江南区队柱路 201 号南宁站（邮政编码：444698）。联系电话：32839928。电子邮箱：jhogr@xqcrazkl.chr.cn

Zhù zhǐ: Jìn Kuān Shǒu Guǎngxī Zhuàngzú Zìzhìqū Nánníng Shì Jiāngnán Qū Duì Zhù Lù 201 Hào Nánníng Zhàn （Yóuzhèng Biānmǎ：444698). Liánxì Diànhuà：32839928. Diànzǐ Yóuxiāng：jhogr@xqcrazkl.chr.cn

Kuan Shou Jin, NanNing Railway Station, 201 Dui Zhu Road, Gangnam District, NanNing, Guangxi Autonomous Region. Postal Code: 444698. Phone Number：32839928. E-mail：jhogr@xqcrazkl.chr.cn

1474。姓名: 阳星禹

住址（博物院）：广西壮族自治区来宾市武宣县锤乙路 753 号来宾博物馆（邮政编码：586874）。联系电话：74184012。电子邮箱：ernsp@itwexfuo.museums.cn

Zhù zhǐ: Yáng Xīng Yǔ Guǎngxī Zhuàngzú Zìzhìqū Láibīn Shì Wǔxuān Xiàn Chuí Yǐ Lù 753 Hào Láibīn Bó Wù Guǎn (Yóuzhèng Biānmǎ：586874). Liánxì Diànhuà：74184012. Diànzǐ Yóuxiāng：ernsp@itwexfuo.museums.cn

Xing Yu Yang, Laibin Museum, 753 Chui Yi Road, Wuxuan County, Laibin, Guangxi Autonomous Region. Postal Code: 586874. Phone Number：74184012. E-mail：ernsp@itwexfuo.museums.cn

1475。姓名: 屠甫圣

住址（湖泊）：广西壮族自治区柳州市三江侗族自治县波土路 693 号钊陆湖（邮政编码：918398）。联系电话：27755221。电子邮箱：ahfjm@ypbfnteo.lakes.cn

Zhù zhǐ: Tú Fǔ Shèng Guǎngxī Zhuàngzú Zìzhìqū Liǔzhōu Shì Sānjiāng Dòngzú Zìzhìxiàn Bō Tǔ Lù 693 Hào Zhāo Lù Hú (Yóuzhèng Biānmǎ：918398). Liánxì Diànhuà：27755221. Diànzǐ Yóuxiāng：ahfjm@ypbfnteo.lakes.cn

Fu Sheng Tu, Zhao Lu Lake, 693 Bo Tu Road, Sanjiang Dong Autonomous County, Liuzhou, Guangxi Autonomous Region. Postal Code: 918398. Phone Number：27755221. E-mail：ahfjm@ypbfnteo.lakes.cn

1476。姓名: 南门源波

住址（大学）：广西壮族自治区梧州市长洲区员不大学洵山路 956 号（邮政编码：199231）。联系电话：56040228。电子邮箱：jpawi@nxwojzau.edu.cn

Zhù zhǐ: Nánmén Yuán Bō Guǎngxī Zhuàngzú Zìzhìqū Wúzhōu Shì Zhǎng Zhōu Qū Yún Bù DàxuéXún Shān Lù 956 Hào (Yóuzhèng Biānmǎ：199231). Liánxì Diànhuà：56040228. Diànzǐ Yóuxiāng：jpawi@nxwojzau.edu.cn

Yuan Bo Nanmen, Yun Bu University, 956 Xun Shan Road, Cheung Chau District, Wuzhou, Guangxi Autonomous Region. Postal Code: 199231. Phone Number：56040228. E-mail：jpawi@nxwojzau.edu.cn

1477。姓名: 樊民民

住址（医院）：广西壮族自治区钦州市灵山县洵水路 343 号奎友医院（邮政编码：411556）。联系电话：73840094。电子邮箱：gnwht@gsxrnbyf.health.cn

Zhù zhǐ: Fán Mín Mín Guǎngxī Zhuàngzú Zìzhìqū Qīnzhōu Shì Língshān Xiàn Xún Shuǐ Lù 343 Hào Kuí Yǒu Yī Yuàn (Yóuzhèng Biānmǎ：411556). Liánxì Diànhuà：73840094. Diànzǐ Yóuxiāng：gnwht@gsxrnbyf.health.cn

Min Min Fan, Kui You Hospital, 343 Xun Shui Road, Lingshan County, Qinzhou, Guangxi Autonomous Region. Postal Code: 411556. Phone Number：73840094. E-mail：gnwht@gsxrnbyf.health.cn

1478。姓名: 钟柱刚

住址（大学）：广西壮族自治区南宁市良庆区轼其大学守威路 775 号（邮政编码：686833）。联系电话：16014759。电子邮箱：kpghx@teqngwpi.edu.cn

Zhù zhǐ: Zhōng Zhù Gāng Guǎngxī Zhuàngzú Zìzhìqū Nánníng Shì Liáng Qìng Qū Shì Qí DàxuéShǒu Wēi Lù 775 Hào (Yóuzhèng Biānmǎ：686833). Liánxì Diànhuà：16014759. Diànzǐ Yóuxiāng：kpghx@teqngwpi.edu.cn

Zhu Gang Zhong, Shi Qi University, 775 Shou Wei Road, Liangqing District, NanNing, Guangxi Autonomous Region. Postal Code: 686833. Phone Number：16014759. E-mail：kpghx@teqngwpi.edu.cn

1479。姓名: 樊陆鹤

住址（公园）：广西壮族自治区柳州市融安县懂南路 148 号帆勇公园（邮政编码：694306）。联系电话：34539913。电子邮箱：updly@vadbmkft.parks.cn

Zhù zhǐ: Fán Lù Hè Guǎngxī Zhuàngzú Zìzhìqū Liǔzhōu Shì Róng Ānxiàn Dǒng Nán Lù 148 Hào Fān Yǒng Gōng Yuán（Yóuzhèng Biānmǎ：694306）. Liánxì Diànhuà：34539913. Diànzǐ Yóuxiāng：updly@vadbmkft.parks.cn

Lu He Fan, Fan Yong Park, 148 Dong Nan Road, Rongan County, Liuzhou, Guangxi Autonomous Region. Postal Code: 694306. Phone Number：34539913. E-mail：updly@vadbmkft.parks.cn

1480。姓名：秋大大

住址（公司）：广西壮族自治区百色市右江区歧宝路 962 号浩焯有限公司（邮政编码：448616）。联系电话：70795020。电子邮箱：tkycv@sjbivfrw.biz.cn

Zhù zhǐ: Qiū Dà Dài Guǎngxī Zhuàngzú Zìzhìqū Bǎisè Shì Yòu Jiāng Qū Qí Bǎo Lù 962 Hào Hào Chāo Yǒuxiàn Gōngsī（Yóuzhèng Biānmǎ：448616）. Liánxì Diànhuà：70795020. Diànzǐ Yóuxiāng：tkycv@sjbivfrw.biz.cn

Da Dai Qiu, Hao Chao Corporation, 962 Qi Bao Road, Youjiang District, Baise, Guangxi Autonomous Region. Postal Code: 448616. Phone Number：70795020. E-mail：tkycv@sjbivfrw.biz.cn

1481。姓名：易涛寰

住址（家庭）：广西壮族自治区贺州市八步区世咚路 313 号强兵公寓 18 层 698 室（邮政编码：784132）。联系电话：43706394。电子邮箱：abvjy@hitofsdp.cn

Zhù zhǐ: Yì Tāo Huán Guǎngxī Zhuàngzú Zìzhìqū Hèzhōu Shì Bā Bù Qū Shì Dōng Lù 313 Hào Qiǎng Bīng Gōng Yù 18 Céng 698 Shì（Yóuzhèng Biānmǎ：784132）. Liánxì Diànhuà：43706394. Diànzǐ Yóuxiāng：abvjy@hitofsdp.cn

Tao Huan Yi, Room# 698, Floor# 18, Qiang Bing Apartment, 313 Shi Dong Road, Babu District, Hezhou, Guangxi Autonomous Region. Postal Code: 784132. Phone Number：43706394. E-mail：abvjy@hitofsdp.cn

1482。姓名: 丰员仲

住址（大学）：广西壮族自治区桂林市雁山区威大大学岐辉路 916 号（邮政编码：602265）。联系电话：85219775。电子邮箱：wnevx@fhydzavt.edu.cn

Zhù zhǐ: Fēng Yún Zhòng Guǎngxī Zhuàngzú Zìzhìqū Guìlín Shì Yàn Shānqū Wēi Dà DàxuéQí Huī Lù 916 Hào（Yóuzhèng Biānmǎ：602265). Liánxì Diànhuà：85219775. Diànzǐ Yóuxiāng：wnevx@fhydzavt.edu.cn

Yun Zhong Feng, Wei Da University, 916 Qi Hui Road, Yanshan District, Guilin, Guangxi Autonomous Region. Postal Code: 602265. Phone Number：85219775. E-mail：wnevx@fhydzavt.edu.cn

1483。姓名: 柴亭大

住址（机场）：广西壮族自治区防城港市上思县福炯路 220 号防城港白葆国际机场（邮政编码：161501）。联系电话：54103630。电子邮箱：yzxsi@clvthnfz.airports.cn

Zhù zhǐ: Chái Tíng Dà Guǎngxī Zhuàngzú Zìzhìqū Fángchénggǎng Shì Shàng Sī Xiàn Fú Jiǒng Lù 220 Hào Fángcénggǎng Bái Bǎo Guó Jì Jī Chǎng（Yóuzhèng Biānmǎ：161501). Liánxì Diànhuà：54103630. Diànzǐ Yóuxiāng：yzxsi@clvthnfz.airports.cn

Ting Da Chai, Fangchenggang Bai Bao International Airport, 220 Fu Jiong Road, Shangsi County, Fangchenggang, Guangxi Autonomous Region. Postal Code: 161501. Phone Number：54103630. E-mail：yzxsi@clvthnfz.airports.cn

1484。姓名: 许星先

住址（机场）：广西壮族自治区玉林市容县领乙路 674 号玉林院珂国际机场（邮政编码：254038）。联系电话：36994275。电子邮箱：latfo@ojumvweh.airports.cn

Zhù zhǐ: Xǔ Xīng Xiān Guǎngxī Zhuàngzú Zìzhìqū Yùlín Shì Róngxiàn Lǐng Yǐ Lù 674 Hào Yùlín Yuàn Kē Guó Jì Jī Chǎng （Yóuzhèng Biānmǎ：254038). Liánxì Diànhuà：36994275. Diànzǐ Yóuxiāng：latfo@ojumvweh.airports.cn

Xing Xian Xu, Yulin Yuan Ke International Airport, 674 Ling Yi Road, Rong County, Yulin, Guangxi Autonomous Region. Postal Code: 254038. Phone Number：36994275. E-mail：latfo@ojumvweh.airports.cn

1485。姓名: 边骥郁

住址（医院）：广西壮族自治区桂林市恭城瑶族自治县王陆路 689 号跃克医院（邮政编码：293466）。联系电话：61909951。电子邮箱：ecjmy@mqhxpisu.health.cn

Zhù zhǐ: Biān Jì Yù Guǎngxī Zhuàngzú Zìzhìqū Guìlín Shì Gōng Chéng Yáozú Zìzhìxiàn Wàng Liù Lù 689 Hào Yuè Kè Yī Yuàn （Yóuzhèng Biānmǎ：293466). Liánxì Diànhuà：61909951. Diànzǐ Yóuxiāng：ecjmy@mqhxpisu.health.cn

Ji Yu Bian, Yue Ke Hospital, 689 Wang Liu Road, Gongcheng Yao Autonomous County, Guilin, Guangxi Autonomous Region. Postal Code: 293466. Phone Number：61909951. E-mail：ecjmy@mqhxpisu.health.cn

1486。姓名: 燕坚中

住址（家庭）：广西壮族自治区贺州市钟山县熔铁路 234 号歧郁公寓 49 层 825 室（邮政编码：816592）。联系电话：72692350。电子邮箱：aplnr@exnkcbws.cn

Zhù zhǐ: Yān Jiān Zhōng Guǎngxī Zhuàngzú Zìzhìqū Hèzhōu Shì Zhōng Shān Xiàn Róng Tiě Lù 234 Hào Qí Yù Gōng Yù 49 Céng 825 Shì (Yóuzhèng Biānmǎ：816592). Liánxì Diànhuà：72692350. Diànzǐ Yóuxiāng：aplnr@exnkcbws.cn

Jian Zhong Yan, Room# 825, Floor# 49, Qi Yu Apartment, 234 Rong Tie Road, Zhongshan County, Hezhou, Guangxi Autonomous Region. Postal Code: 816592. Phone Number：72692350. E-mail：aplnr@exnkcbws.cn

1487。姓名：仉督陆奎

住址（公园）：广西壮族自治区贵港市桂平市斌全路 514 号敬圣公园（邮政编码：554421）。联系电话：68790886。电子邮箱：dywlf@jdmaerpl.parks.cn

Zhù zhǐ: Zhǎngdū Lù Kuí Guǎngxī Zhuàngzú Zìzhìqū Guìgǎng Shì Guìpíngshì Bīn Quán Lù 514 Hào Jìng Shèng Gōng Yuán（Yóuzhèng Biānmǎ：554421). Liánxì Diànhuà：68790886. Diànzǐ Yóuxiāng：dywlf@jdmaerpl.parks.cn

Lu Kui Zhangdu, Jing Sheng Park, 514 Bin Quan Road, Guiping, Guigang, Guangxi Autonomous Region. Postal Code: 554421. Phone Number：68790886. E-mail：dywlf@jdmaerpl.parks.cn

1488。姓名：充中庆

住址（大学）：广西壮族自治区桂林市阳朔县红绅大学葛秀路 260 号（邮政编码：264444）。联系电话：57878259。电子邮箱：guhkr@gcpqzrtk.edu.cn

Zhù zhǐ: Chōng Zhōng Qìng Guǎngxī Zhuàngzú Zìzhìqū Guìlín Shì Yángshuò Xiàn Hóng Shēn DàxuéGé Xiù Lù 260 Hào（Yóuzhèng Biānmǎ：264444). Liánxì Diànhuà：57878259. Diànzǐ Yóuxiāng：guhkr@gcpqzrtk.edu.cn

Zhong Qing Chong, Hong Shen University, 260 Ge Xiu Road, Yangshuo County, Guilin, Guangxi Autonomous Region. Postal Code: 264444. Phone Number：57878259. E-mail：guhkr@gcpqzrtk.edu.cn

1489。姓名：莘焯仲

住址（火车站）：广西壮族自治区桂林市象山区咚鹤路 207 号桂林站（邮政编码：762830）。联系电话：17650359。电子邮箱：aqhxj@sjbghauf.chr.cn

Zhù zhǐ: Shēn Chāo Zhòng Guǎngxī Zhuàngzú Zìzhìqū Guìlín Shì Xiàngshānqū Dōng Hè Lù 207 Hào Gulín Zhàn（Yóuzhèng Biānmǎ：762830). Liánxì Diànhuà：17650359. Diànzǐ Yóuxiāng：aqhxj@sjbghauf.chr.cn

Chao Zhong Shen, Guilin Railway Station, 207 Dong He Road, Xiangshan District, Guilin, Guangxi Autonomous Region. Postal Code: 762830. Phone Number：17650359. E-mail：aqhxj@sjbghauf.chr.cn

1490。姓名: 萧炯盛

住址（公共汽车站）：广西壮族自治区桂林市恭城瑶族自治县坡坤路 999 号顺全站（邮政编码：239694）。联系电话：16851371。电子邮箱：maxjk@mowxfbdu.transport.cn

Zhù zhǐ: Xiāo Jiǒng Chéng Guǎngxī Zhuàngzú Zìzhìqū Guìlín Shì Gōng Chéng Yáozú Zìzhìxiàn Pō Kūn Lù 999 Hào Shùn Quán Zhàn (Yóuzhèng Biānmǎ：239694). Liánxì Diànhuà：16851371. Diànzǐ Yóuxiāng：maxjk@mowxfbdu.transport.cn

Jiong Cheng Xiao, Shun Quan Bus Station, 999 Po Kun Road, Gongcheng Yao Autonomous County, Guilin, Guangxi Autonomous Region. Postal Code: 239694. Phone Number：16851371. E-mail：maxjk@mowxfbdu.transport.cn

1491。姓名: 伊恩学

住址（公园）：广西壮族自治区钦州市钦南区继游路 513 号易祥公园（邮政编码：242400）。联系电话：75958022。电子邮箱：cjisq@lxdjzypg.parks.cn

Zhù zhǐ: Yī Ēn Xué Guǎngxī Zhuàngzú Zìzhìqū Qīnzhōu Shì Qīn Nán Qū Jì Yóu Lù 513 Hào Yì Xiáng Gōng Yuán (Yóuzhèng Biānmǎ：242400). Liánxì Diànhuà：75958022. Diànzǐ Yóuxiāng：cjisq@lxdjzypg.parks.cn

En Xue Yi, Yi Xiang Park, 513 Ji You Road, Chennan District, Qinzhou, Guangxi Autonomous Region. Postal Code: 242400. Phone Number：75958022. E-mail：cjisq@lxdjzypg.parks.cn

1492。姓名: 解立豪

住址（公园）：广西壮族自治区贵港市港南区南继路 565 号歧福公园（邮政编码：299846）。联系电话：65610945。电子邮箱：barvz@qkzwgsef.parks.cn

Zhù zhǐ: Xiè Lì Háo Guǎngxī Zhuàngzú Zìzhìqū Guìgǎng Shì Gǎngnán Qū Nán Jì Lù 565 Hào Qí Fú Gōng Yuán (Yóuzhèng Biānmǎ: 299846). Liánxì Diànhuà: 65610945. Diànzǐ Yóuxiāng: barvz@qkzwgsef.parks.cn

Li Hao Xie, Qi Fu Park, 565 Nan Ji Road, Konan District, Guigang, Guangxi Autonomous Region. Postal Code: 299846. Phone Number: 65610945. E-mail: barvz@qkzwgsef.parks.cn

1493。姓名: 毕顺化

住址（博物院）：广西壮族自治区梧州市藤县易翰路 160 号梧州博物馆（邮政编码：274820）。联系电话：94521977。电子邮箱：jrqxs@ekbvzjtd.museums.cn

Zhù zhǐ: Bì Shùn Huā Guǎngxī Zhuàngzú Zìzhìqū Wúzhōu Shì Téng Xiàn Yì Hàn Lù 160 Hào Wúzōu Bó Wù Guǎn (Yóuzhèng Biānmǎ: 274820). Liánxì Diànhuà: 94521977. Diànzǐ Yóuxiāng: jrqxs@ekbvzjtd.museums.cn

Shun Hua Bi, Wuzhou Museum, 160 Yi Han Road, Fuji County, Wuzhou, Guangxi Autonomous Region. Postal Code: 274820. Phone Number: 94521977. E-mail: jrqxs@ekbvzjtd.museums.cn

1494。姓名: 嵇乙亭

住址（家庭）：广西壮族自治区贵港市港南区敬星路 247 号翰可公寓 14 层 629 室（邮政编码：792390）。联系电话：63668513。电子邮箱：kmuen@nobltwrp.cn

Zhù zhǐ: Jī Yǐ Tíng Guǎngxī Zhuàngzú Zìzhìqū Guìgǎng Shì Gǎngnán Qū Jìng Xīng Lù 247 Hào Hàn Kě Gōng Yù 14 Céng 629 Shì (Yóuzhèng Biānmǎ: 792390). Liánxì Diànhuà: 63668513. Diànzǐ Yóuxiāng: kmuen@nobltwrp.cn

Yi Ting Ji, Room# 629, Floor# 14, Han Ke Apartment, 247 Jing Xing Road, Konan District, Guigang, Guangxi Autonomous Region. Postal Code: 792390. Phone Number: 63668513. E-mail: kmuen@nobltwrp.cn

1495。姓名: 上官冠陆

住址（公园）: 广西壮族自治区贺州市八步区锡近路 731 号化游公园（邮政编码: 607323）。联系电话: 43013944。电子邮箱: zjirs@xqvarhsp.parks.cn

Zhù zhǐ: Shàngguān Guàn Liù Guǎngxī Zhuàngzú Zìzhìqū Hèzhōu Shì Bā Bù Qū Xī Jìn Lù 731 Hào Huā Yóu Gōng Yuán（Yóuzhèng Biānmǎ: 607323）. Liánxì Diànhuà: 43013944. Diànzǐ Yóuxiāng: zjirs@xqvarhsp.parks.cn

Guan Liu Shangguan, Hua You Park, 731 Xi Jin Road, Babu District, Hezhou, Guangxi Autonomous Region. Postal Code: 607323. Phone Number: 43013944. E-mail: zjirs@xqvarhsp.parks.cn

1496。姓名: 乜学辙

住址（公司）: 广西壮族自治区百色市德保县俊食路 580 号化铁有限公司（邮政编码: 114903）。联系电话: 14169861。电子邮箱: zysqw@elnizbdu.biz.cn

Zhù zhǐ: Niè Xué Zhé Guǎngxī Zhuàngzú Zìzhìqū Bǎisè Shì Dé Bǎo Xiàn Jùn Yì Lù 580 Hào Huā Fū Yǒuxiàn Gōngsī（Yóuzhèng Biānmǎ: 114903）. Liánxì Diànhuà: 14169861. Diànzǐ Yóuxiāng: zysqw@elnizbdu.biz.cn

Xue Zhe Nie, Hua Fu Corporation, 580 Jun Yi Road, Debao County, Baise, Guangxi Autonomous Region. Postal Code: 114903. Phone Number: 14169861. E-mail: zysqw@elnizbdu.biz.cn

1497。姓名: 第五坚毅

住址（火车站）: 广西壮族自治区河池市环江毛南族自治县葛毅路 216 号河池站（邮政编码: 569577）。联系电话: 19994177。电子邮箱: oegtd@zryvdpal.chr.cn

Zhù zhǐ: Dìwǔ Jiān Yì Guǎngxī Zhuàngzú Zìzhìqū Héchí Shì Huán Jiāng Máonán Zú Zìzhìxiàn Gé Yì Lù 216 Hào Hécí Zhàn（Yóuzhèng Biānmǎ: 569577）. Liánxì Diànhuà: 19994177. Diànzǐ Yóuxiāng: oegtd@zryvdpal.chr.cn

Jian Yi Diwu, Hechi Railway Station, 216 Ge Yi Road, Huanjiang Maonan Autonomous County, Hechi, Guangxi Autonomous Region. Postal Code: 569577. Phone Number：19994177. E-mail：oegtd@zryvdpal.chr.cn

1498。姓名: 欧阳智白

住址（火车站）：广西壮族自治区柳州市融安县继豹路 972 号柳州站（邮政编码：893509）。联系电话：35260754。电子邮箱：djcmp@vdkofrlq.chr.cn

Zhù zhǐ: Ōuyáng Zhì Bái Guǎngxī Zhuàngzú Zìzhìqū Liǔzhōu Shì Róng Ānxiàn Jì Bào Lù 972 Hào Liǔzōu Zhàn (Yóuzhèng Biānmǎ：893509). Liánxì Diànhuà：35260754. Diànzǐ Yóuxiāng：djcmp@vdkofrlq.chr.cn

Zhi Bai Ouyang, Liuzhou Railway Station, 972 Ji Bao Road, Rongan County, Liuzhou, Guangxi Autonomous Region. Postal Code: 893509. Phone Number：35260754. E-mail：djcmp@vdkofrlq.chr.cn

1499。姓名: 危领泽

住址（公司）：广西壮族自治区钦州市钦北区葛顺路 930 号恩柱有限公司（邮政编码：279630）。联系电话：34385514。电子邮箱：ghsbc@gufzwsyl.biz.cn

Zhù zhǐ: Wēi Lǐng Zé Guǎngxī Zhuàngzú Zìzhìqū Qīnzhōu Shì Qīn Běi Qū Gé Shùn Lù 930 Hào Ēn Zhù Yǒuxiàn Gōngsī (Yóuzhèng Biānmǎ：279630). Liánxì Diànhuà：34385514. Diànzǐ Yóuxiāng：ghsbc@gufzwsyl.biz.cn

Ling Ze Wei, En Zhu Corporation, 930 Ge Shun Road, Qinbei District, Qinzhou, Guangxi Autonomous Region. Postal Code: 279630. Phone Number：34385514. E-mail：ghsbc@gufzwsyl.biz.cn

1500。姓名: 华祥冕

住址（公园）：广西壮族自治区贺州市八步区桥锤路 198 号超仲公园（邮政编码：272366）。联系电话：39800283。电子邮箱：nkqbz@arewfdzx.parks.cn

Zhù zhǐ: Huà Xiáng Miǎn Guǎngxī Zhuàngzú Zìzhìqū Hèzhōu Shì Bā Bù Qū Qiáo Chuí Lù 198 Hào Chāo Zhòng Gōng Yuán (Yóuzhèng Biānmǎ：272366). Liánxì Diànhuà：39800283. Diànzǐ Yóuxiāng：nkqbz@arewfdzx.parks.cn

Xiang Mian Hua, Chao Zhong Park, 198 Qiao Chui Road, Babu District, Hezhou, Guangxi Autonomous Region. Postal Code: 272366. Phone Number：39800283. E-mail：nkqbz@arewfdzx.parks.cn

Milton Keynes UK
Ingram Content Group UK Ltd.
UKHW030205011223
433552UK00013B/454